Spiritual Psychology

The Twelve Primary Life Lessons

Information for Facilitators of Human Evolution

Spiritual Psychology

The Twelve Primary Life Lessons

Published by: **Lightworker**

P.O. Box 1496
Poway Ca. 92074-1496 USA
www.Lightworker.com
LWPub@Lightworker.com

Lightworker Books and Tapes and DVD's can be purchased in finer retail stores, on the internet at www.lightworker.com, or by contacting Lightworker at country code 01 800 248 5837

Spiritual Psychology ~ The Twelve Primary Life Lessons
By Steve Rother
Edited by Sandra Sedgbeer
Cover Design Steven Morris
Morris Creative, San Diego Ca. www.thinkfeelwork.com
Book Layout by Steve Hansen, UK. Dreamstonedesigns.com
Fig 6-7 Illustration by Cathy Sargent, all others by the Author
Copyright © 2004 – Steve Rother
Printed in the USA
First Edition - First Printing – June 2004

ISBN 1928806-10-4

Table of Contents

Introduction

A right brain approach to a left brain world.

Have you ever wondered why some people grow up in what might appear to be the perfect life circumstances with the ideal, supportive parents, yet they just can't seem to master the simple things in life?

Have you ever known someone who, despite being highly intelligent, keeps on repeating the same mistakes over and over again in their life?

And how about the people who just seem to have been born lucky? Or, conversely, someone who, despite all their efforts to change things, just seems to be plain *unlucky*?

Some believe that we are a product of our environment. According to others, who we are, and how we turn out, is largely dictated by our genetic structure (the nature versus nurture debate). It could equally be claimed that, just like a pendulum, each generation naturally does the very opposite of what its parents and role models did. But that doesn't always fit either.

It is only when we begin to view the human experience as the evolutionary process of a soul that we can begin to understand all the strange forces at work in our lives.

We see ourselves as human beings searching for a spiritual awakening when, in fact, we are spiritual beings trying to cope with a human awakening. But what causes us, as spiritual beings, to seek this human experience in the first place? What is it, precisely, that sets certain life patterns into motion? And why and how do these patterns emerge in our own behaviors?

The answers to these, and many other baffling questions, are what this book is all about. In these pages, you will discover a very different view of life and the human experience than you have been taught elsewhere.

The truth is, we learn through repetition. Thus, the patterns that repeat themselves in our lives reveal much more information about us, and the life lessons we came here to work on, than we can possibly imagine. What's more, understanding these patterns is not only critical to understanding ourselves, it also can create widespread changes in our life.

In many instances, merely understanding the 'why' of things is sufficient to effect positive and permanent changes. In these times of uncertainty, when things are changing virtually on a daily basis, it has become more important than ever for us to understand the *whys* of our lives. This is especially true for facilitators who play a front line role in helping others to achieve mastery over the pain and problems of their past, so that they can create a happier and healthier future.

Generally, when a facilitator spots repetitive negative patterns in a client's life, he or she immediately attempts to interpret the underlying cause or reason for repeating the negative action or behavior. Although this can be helpful for some people in some cases, it does not offer any satisfactory explanation as to why those patterns existed in the first place. It is here that most facilitators will look for early imprints from a life experience that may have made a person behave in a particular manner, and then help the person to change the belief system that created the unwanted patterns. But this is only part of the answer. What if there is a much higher purpose behind these behavioral patterns? And what would happen if we could find ways of identifying this higher purpose and in so doing turn seemingly destructive patterns into positive attributes? The answer to these questions and more are presented in the following pages.

The story of how this book came into being is still more than I can comprehend at times. Let me state right up front, I have no traditional credentials to back up what I am about to reveal. If credentials are important to you, then you may not be entirely comfortable with this material. Neither would I have been if I'd received this information ten years ago. Believe me, I never dreamed I would be working in the arena of Spiritual Psychology. Until eight years ago, I was very comfortable in my life as a building contractor. I thought I knew what I was going to be when I grew up. I liked what I did because it gave me a real sense of accomplishment and creativity. Still, somewhere in the back of my head, I knew there was something more I had to do.

Then one day I started receiving what I call *divinely inspired* information from a collective of angelic spirits simply known as 'the Group.' This caused great upheaval in all areas of my life. Marriage, family, finances, business and my entire perspective of myself changed dramatically. Despite all the upheaval this caused, and all the challenges for me and my wife, for the first time in my life I felt I had truly found my passion. Deep inside, I knew that the information I was receiving was truth. The profound changes that occurred as a result of this experience could easily fill a book. However, not this one. Hopefully this explains how a contractor came to be writing about spiritual psychology.

Receiving divinely inspired information is not as unusual as you may think. Some people regard this as New Age psychobabble. Others simply call it mediumship, or channeling. Regardless of your viewpoint, we all have a connection to a higher part of ourselves, which provides us with divine inspiration. Most people just have not learned to trust it. Artists call it 'inspiration.' Writers say they are 'in the flow.' Baseball players say they are 'in the groove,' and the musician is 'plugged in.' These are the special times when we connect with our own higher self. This is what I have learned to do on a regular basis, and I simply call my connection 'the Group.'*

I offer this information not as a definitive source, but rather, as a new perspective on the human experience that may assist you in changing your life for the better. Thus, though it may not provide all the answers you seek, I hope that it will at least leave you with new questions to ponder. As is my philosophy of life, take from it what you can, and use only what works for you.

Over the past eight years, I have personally conducted over six thousand private sessions in which I assist people to see their life patterns from the higher perspective of the Group. I neither diagnose, nor prescribe treatment for any condition or ailment. I do not do crisis counseling, nor do I ever dictate what anyone should do. That was the old paradigm where people looked outside themselves for answers. What I offer is simply an opportunity to perceive life from a different perspective. My intent is to help you re-member what you already know as a spiritual being having a human experience.

The information I receive is not about the Group per se, it is about human empowerment. Nor is the Group discussed in this material except as a referenced source. If you would like to find out more from the Group, This information is available in other books and on the web site Lightworker.com.

Assumptions made in this Book

It is important to know that the material in this book is based on a number of assumptions that form an integral part of this information. I offer these concepts for your information and invite you to use your own discernment when putting them into use.

1. There is an assumed belief that we are actually spiritual beings experiencing life in human form.

2. There is an assumed belief that we are simply energy, which can never die but can only change forms. Thus, there are many references to reincarnation in this work.

3. There is an intrinsic belief that we experience life within a field of polarity, therefore, we see ourselves as separate from one another when, in reality, we are inseparable. Thus, concepts of good and bad, right and wrong, black and white, love and fear, etc. are all illusions of polarity.

4. There is an understanding that humanity is undergoing a quantum leap in our evolution, causing us to seek higher truths to support our newly heightened state of existence.

5. There is an understanding that the human spirit is an incredibly powerful force of creation, and as such, life is simply a self-fulfilling prophecy.

I sincerely hope that the concepts presented here will improve your life in some way. In today's rapidly evolving world, success is no longer defined in the traditional manner. It is defined by how much passion and joy each one of us can experience on a daily basis. I hope this material enables you to discover a little more of your own passion and joy.

Intuition

All of the information presented in this book is from a spiritual perspective. This simply means that we must first deal with what is happening on a spiritual level before we can effect change in our physical world. Utilizing this information requires us to use greater intuition. This is not as difficult as people think. I firmly believe that we all have access to these natural abilities, it's just that many people do not trust the information they receive. Those involved in the healing arts have a better grasp of these concepts, as the work they do often requires them to trust their intuitive abilities.

We have all experienced times when we 'know' something without knowing how we know it. Or we find ourselves saying something without knowing where the words came from. This is intuition. This is channeling. And there is nothing mysterious or unnatural about it. If we don't trust it, or we get scared and shut it off, we are closing down our connection to our internal guidance system, which is a fundamental part of ourselves.

This book provides you with a framework in which you can learn to trust and develop this ability.

Dedication

To the Catalysts in my Life.

Throughout this work you will find many references to the catalyst in every person's life who is responsible for activating their life lesson. Generally this is done by a parent or someone very close to them in childhood. These people have tremendous influence in our lives. It feels appropriate here to tell you an unusual story about the catalysts in my own life since this book is dedicated to them.

All my life I was very close to my mother. She had an uncanny ability to see right through me. No matter what smoke screen I tried to erect, she always knew when I was trying to fool others, as well as when I was kidding myself. I could always count on her to help me gain the proper perspective on my life. More than anyone, my mom taught me how to be in integrity with myself.

Mom always believed she was meant to be a writer. It was her dream to write her life story and share all her most important discoveries with the world. She was always writing articles and submitting them to her favorite magazines. Although her wisdom would have been a real gift to the world, I don't think she ever found her 'voice' in her writings. She was published only once that I am aware of. It was an article that she wrote about my wedding to Barbara over 30 years ago. Barbara had lost her own mother when she was very young and my mom loved her as her own daughter. The article was entitled "Mother of the Bride *and* Groom."

Mom died young from breast cancer. She was only 53. That is the same age I am at the time of this writting. At the time she died I did not have the understandings of life that I have now. Although she laid the groundwork for much of the spiritual understandings I still hold today, I wasn't really into this work at that time. Still, I knew in my heart that even though she died very young, Mom had completed what she came here to do. Shortly before she died she found happiness in a new marriage following a difficult divorce from my father. Despite everything, she never stopped loving Dad. Even though it was difficult for her, she never fell into victim mentality. She took her power and found happiness in a new love relationship. She and my stepfather had been married for just a year when she left us.

I will never forget going up to her writing room a few days after her death. Her brand new typewriter sat on a beautiful desk placed in front of the window. This was where she had planned to write her story. File folders in her desk drawer were filled with partially written ideas and the book she had begun only months before. I sat down at her desk, put my fingers on the typewriter keys and stared out the window, trying to imagine what it would be like to write.

My father was a profound dreamer who had an astonishing ability to create anything he set his mind to. He had a love for life, and for people, which touched everyone with whom he came in contact. He was a larger-than-life character. Everyone loved Jack. Even though he left us years ago, his corny sense of humor is still heard at every family gathering. When someone in the family recites one of his overused jokes we all accuse them of 'channeling' Dad. We joke about it, but we feel him with us all the time. It's as if he is just over our shoulders, whispering in our ears, reminding us of a corny joke that we must have heard a million times.

Dad loved helping others. People from all walks of life sought him out to discuss their problems. He never refused anyone. We used to joke that he had earned his degree in 'kitchen table counseling,' even though his actual college degree was in electrical engineering. Later in life he decided to study as a psychologist and start living his dream, doing what he loved as a professional counselor and seminar leader. Dad had completed all his courses and was working on the final component of his thesis for a Ph.D. in psychology when he died. Although I was not into his 'weird' encounter groups and seminars at the time, he often talked about the breakthroughs people had made in them. He loved to teach and to help people grow. Even so, he had a very difficult time making a living doing the work he so loved. Looking back, I can see that he was just ahead of his time. In fact, I dedicated my first book to him as a Lightworker slightly ahead of his time.

When I first started this work, he took me to lunch one day, and in a very loving manner, he tried to tell me how hard it might be for me to make a living doing this work. I listened to what he said, but as with all young men who think they are somehow different than their parents, I went ahead anyway. The last Christmas we had together, I was able to share with him that I had just been invited to speak to a group at the United Nations in Vienna, Austria. He was really happy for me, and I somehow felt a sense of completion in him that I did not quite understand at the time.

Even at 73, Dad still rode his motorcycle every day and played tennis, which was his first true love. He always played mixed doubles because that way, he said, he got to flirt with good looking girls. He always told us that when he died it would either be on the tennis court or in bed with a beautiful blonde. At the time of his death he was in his second marriage to a very attractive blonde. And, just as he had scripted, he died right after sharing a "high five" with his attractive female partner upon winning a set point on the tennis court.

I share these stories here because, as a parent myself, I know that the very best I can hope for from my children is that they will adopt something I was passionate about and take it a step further than I did. My mother was an unpublished author, and my father was a psychologist and teacher who never really got the chance to put his passion into practice. I have no doubt that the roles I asked them to play in my life when I scripted it were perfectly aligned to set the stage for the work I now am blessed to do. My parents did a great job as my catalysts, and I have no doubt that they are always just over my shoulder, watching and smiling.

Chapter 1

The Twelve Paradigms

―――――――

Suggestions for Healing

in a New World

Healer =

One who creates space for others to feel comfortable enough to heal themselves.

In days past if people were ill or needed healing of any kind they would always look to a facilitator or healer. They walked in looking for quick-fix answers; a pill, a diet or any magic potion that would help them heal. This worked quite well up to this point in our evolution. It allowed us to get the help we think we need. Even the old-time faith healers would only be required to touch someone for a healing to take place. I myself have been credited with saving several lives. I do not discount these 'miracles' in any way, as I know the power that a spirit has to heal the body it inhabits. In all of these cases, what is really happening is that the facilitator is doing what is necessary to give the client permission to heal themselves. When patients see the dramatic result, they automatically acclaim the facilitator as a gifted healer or miracle worker.

The challenge, now that we are learning to become fully empowered humans, is that it is no longer appropriate for us to give our power away to anyone else, including healers and facilitators. This is a drastic change in the overall perception of, and paradigm for, facilitation in general. As a result, we are seeing new healing paradigms emerge almost daily. What follows is a list of suggestions for working with people in the new energy of self-empowerment. None of these are new ideas, nor are they designed to be rules that must be steadfastly adhered to. Rather, they are intended to act as a reminder to facilitators that we are now in a time of dealing with the empowered human.

The Latin phrase "Primum non nocere" translated to: First do no harm. is attributed to Hippocrates, widely known as the father of medicine. Now that we are living in the age of empowerment, it is time to take this one stage further – i.e., to find a way to facilitate your client's healing *without taking their power from them.*

What follows are twelve suggestions that were given to me as I started this work. The 12 Paradigms for Facilitation are intended to help you to define higher truths for yourself, and keep your balance while creating space for others to heal themselves.

1. Focus on Empowerment
Healing in the higher vibrations of the New Earth can only take place when people hold their own power. This means that our first concern and our first intent must always be to find ways to facilitate others without taking their power from them.

2. Healing by Request
All healing facilitation must be by request only. It is no longer possible to facilitate healing for others without their specifically requesting it.

3. Intent
In the New Energy, it is only possible to facilitate healing with the highest intent. As we further evolve we will find that there are no more secrets. Thus, as facilitators, we must allow ourselves and our motivations to be fully apparent.

4. Perception
Understand that illness is not always a sign that something is wrong. There are times when illness is necessary to facilitate change, and our role is merely to help facilitate that process. It's important to recognize that illness is only one state of health, and that a healing facilitator must learn to work with all states in order to create space where health prevails.

5. Truth
As a facilitator, it is important to speak one's own truth.

Yet, in doing so, we must acknowledge that truth is always a work in progress. Thus, leave yourself room for growth in the words you speak, and speak your truth in a fashion that allows others to stand in their own truth without feeling threatened by yours. Honor all flavors of the truth, no matter how different they may seem from your own. Remember - competition is only an illusion of the polarity in which we live.

6. Balanced Ego
A balanced ego is necessary in order to facilitate healing. Thus, as facilitators, it is necessary for us to check our egos often and to examine truthfully our own motivations for our actions or words. If our ego grows too big, it will cut us off from our source. Yet, if it is not big enough, we will never take our place as facilitators.

7. Discernment
We must learn to practice the art of discernment in making choices without judgment; to monitor carefully what enters our field and to be discriminating about choosing only those things and ideas that complement us. Everything else should be released without judgment. We do not have to be a part of everything. Rather, we must learn to choose only what feeds and nurtures *us*.

8. Creating Safe Space
The wisest words that a facilitator can use are: **"I do not know."** Thus, even as we are teaching, we must make space for the empowerment of others. None of us has all of the answers, but together, all of us have access to all of the answers.

9. Vulnerability
Our true strength as healers lies in being able to be vulnerable. It is our humanness that makes us special. We must learn to let this shine through in all that we do,

and to share mistakes openly with others. In this way, our perceived weaknesses will soon become our greatest strengths.

10. Mastery of Thought
Remember - we may not have control over the thoughts that enter our heads, but we do have complete control over what stays there. Thus it is our responsibility to become a master of our own thoughts and to share this process with those with whom we work.

11. Motivation
It is important to understand that everyone has the same base motivation. Fundamentally, we are all like little children, fumbling around in a darkened room, searching for the door back into the light. The easiest way to find the Light while not hurting one another is to hold hands.

12. Responsibility
It is not possible to heal another. It is only possible to create and to offer them the space in which to heal themselves, if they so choose. So do not take responsibility for the healing of anyone other than you. If you should find yourself drained of energy by your clients it is because you are taking responsibility for their healing. Remember that responsibility is the balance of power. Help those you facilitate to take responsibility for their own healing so that they may hold their true power.

Facilitating healing is highly honored work. But let us never forget one golden rule:

> Heal another and you may change their life.
> Help another to heal themselves and you will change the Universe.

Chapter 2

The Art
of
Mastery

Mastering Life through
Mastering Life Lessons

Mastery is an Inside Job.

All life lessons are always focused inward. If the life lesson is Definition, it's about defining your own boundaries and not those of others. If it's a life lesson of Acceptance, it's never about accepting what is around you, it's about accepting yourself. Likewise, in a life lesson of Trust, it is not about trusting other people, it's about trusting yourself. We are all responsible for ourselves, and so this is where we will find the direction of any life lesson. There is a saying: we cannot change another person; we can only change ourselves. This is not entirely true. But as you will see when you read the section on redefining the role of the catalyst below, this is the only place that we can focus our intent when it comes to life lessons.

The Art of Mastery

It's important to note that we all work with all of these attributes every day. The act of mastery does not mean that we will never have a problem with any of these again. Likewise, mastering a life lesson does not mean that we will 'walk on water' in that area. What it means is that the particular attribute we are working on will cease to be a problem in our lives.

Why is it that some people who were raised by loving, caring parents and are full of integrity themselves often have children who appear to be markedly lacking in this attribute and spend their entire lives having problems with issues of integrity? And why do others, who appear to have the perfect role models for integrity problems, often seem to grow up with a natural sense of balance in this area? The answer is simply that the latter individual may have already mastered the life lesson of Integrity. Mastery is not something that is necessarily easy to identify, since all it means is that, once mastered, that particular attribute is simply not an issue in subsequent lifetimes.

As mentioned in the chapter on Energy Matrix – Energy Stamps, when people master a life lesson that is being facilitated through an energy stamp, it relieves them from the challenges associated with that particular life lesson. They either rewrite the script, and heal the energy stamp, or they change it. In other words, when a life lesson that is facilitated by an energy stamp is mastered, the difficult habits, challenges, or behavioral patterns associated with it seem to leave the person as their life changes for the better. While the same is true of a person working with an energy matrix, however, the innate wiring never changes.

For example, people working with an energy matrix in a life lesson of Definition are naturally wired to attract master manipulators into their lives. If a girl in this situation enters a room full of men, the ones she is naturally most attracted to will invariably turn out to be major manipulators. Now, even though she may master this life lesson and learn to define her boundaries effortlessly and quickly, she will still be 'wired' to attract master manipulators. And she will remain so throughout her entire lifetime. The difference now, however, is that she will have become very good at identifying them and will know what she needs to do in order to change the energy.

It's important to bear in mind that neither the master manipulator in this scenario, nor the girl who has the problem of defining her boundaries, are bad people. It's simply the way their life lessons interact with each other's. In the case of the girl, she probably feels as though she has a sign on her forehead saying: "*I have weak boundaries, come push them!*" Even after she has mastered this attribute, she will still have that metaphoric sign on her forehead, and will still be transmitting the same message, but it will no longer be so easy for her to be manipulated. In her next lifetime, this will no longer be a problem for her, but she might wonder why it keeps to happening to her best friend.

This is what mastery looks like according to the Group.

Although it is not common for us to re-work a primary life lesson once it has been mastered, since we are spiritual beings having a human experience on the planet of free choice, it is entirely possible that even after we have reached a level of mastery with a particular life attribute, we may still fall back into old patterns. Generally, when we do take a backward step, it is likely to be a small one, and is usually recognized very quickly. It's actually very rare for a person to spend an entire lifetime re-working a life lesson that's already been mastered.

When helping people identify their life lessons and the contracts associated with them, it's very important for facilitators to resist the temptation to jump to conclusions based on one or two experiences or incidents that the client may relate.

Of all the people whom I have helped to identify their life lessons, the most difficult for me to identify have been those who have already attained a measure of mastery. Of these, it has been much easier to identify a person working with an energy matrix as opposed to an energy stamp.

According to the Group, the definition of mastery is *the act of taking something negative and using it in a positive way.* For instance, imagine that there is a line of life energy, much like a straight line, traveling across your timeline of human experience. We expend a lot of our energy trying to keep these energy lines straight. Since success (or health) is represented by a constant straight line of life force energy, we feel uncomfortable when that line wavers or has spikes in it.

As facilitators, we are trained to view illness, sickness and disease as signs of something being wrong. The 12 Paradigms of Facilitation teaches us that all illness is a process. Consequently, if we can facilitate the process, we can help the patient. As in our illustration of the energy lines, when we witness dips or fluctuations in client's energy lines, we immediately rush to their aid, to help them return their energy line to its natural healthy position. Not only is this usually a slow process; it's one that, ultimately, can only be accomplished by the clients themselves.

One clue that can be helpful to facilitators is to look at each spike or drop in the client's energy line as a possibility for mastery. In other words, instead of trying to return their energy line to its normal position, it would be more helpful to show them where a negative situation can be used in a positive manner. Taking each emotional condition, illness, energy dip or setback as a potential opportunity for mastery is a wonderful way for us to raise our own usefulness as healing facilitators.

We've all heard stories of psychologists who went into the profession as a direct result of the abuse issues they themselves suffered as children. Or the surgeon whose burning desire to become a doctor stemmed from seeing his mother die of cancer. These are perfect examples of mastery. Mastery has many faces, so it's important to look for them all when working with a client.

The Teacher Emerges

Whenever people reach a level of mastery in any life lesson, they invariably move into some form of teaching. There are two interesting things to note about this. Firstly, they rarely teach anything related to their own life lesson. Instead, they usually teach in some other area of their passion. Secondly, this is rarely a formal or even conscious move towards teaching. In most cases, the students just start showing up. What happens is that other people appear to start seeking them out, wanting to be around them more in order to learn from them. It's as if, having attained a level of mastery in their particular life lesson, the teacher within them just naturally emerges.

Changing the Role of the Catalyst

The other thing that happens when any level of mastery is attained is that our relationship with the catalyst in our life also changes. Take the case of Lee, for example. Lee was clearly working with a life lesson of Trust. Her father, who had abused her physically and emotionally, was the negative catalyst in her life. Whenever Lee talks about her father today, it is with a sense of sadness. It's not that she is sad for herself. On the contrary, she and her father actually have a very strong bond that goes far beyond any event in one lifetime. Thus, Lee not only loves her father unconditionally, she also knows him better than he knows himself. What makes her sad are the poor choices her father has made in his life, and the fact that even though she knows he really loves her, he has never been able to express that love in words. After two marriages and two divorces, Lee is now mastering her life lesson of Trust. As with all life lessons, this is focused inward. So, after a lifetime of having the rug pulled out from under her feet, and having to deal with untrustworthy people, Lee is finally learning to trust herself. She may not necessarily be aware that things are changing for her, but she is no longer hesitating to take charge of situations, trust her own decisions, and not be afraid of making mistakes. For the first time in her life, Lee is taking responsibility for what happens to her, and it feels good.

Lee is estranged from her parents. Following her divorce, she not only found it really hard to be around them for long periods of time, she also felt it was important to put her own needs first. Although they have had some contact in the past two years, it has been minimal, and never for more than a few minutes at a time.

Once she started to trust herself, and to not be afraid to act on that trust, her life started rapidly changing. One day, out of the blue, Lee's father called her and said that he missed her, that he would like to talk, and could they have lunch one day. Although this was out of character, Lee decided to go along and hear what her father had to say. Perhaps he was beginning to mellow with age, she thought, and now was feeling some regrets and wanting to make amends. She knew he couldn't bring himself to tell her he loved her, so perhaps, in his mind, this was the next best thing. When it came to their lunch date, however, Lee's father simply chit-chatted about various matters, quite normally, as if it had been just yesterday since they had last seen one another, and when it was time to leave, he shocked her by saying, "I love ya, honey," as if he had been saying it for years.

Now, if you were to ask Lee and her father what had happened in this situation, both would very likely tell you that the other had changed. In fact, what was really happening here was that as Lee began mastering her life lesson of Trust, she also began to redefine the role her father played in her life. Since she no longer needed him to act as a catalyst, unbeknown to either of them on a conscious level, she had released him from the need to play his former role.

Redefining the art of mastery means reevaluating our attitudes towards all potentially negative situations. Fearlessly searching for potentials in all situations can quickly transform any situation, and looking for every opportunity to use a negative event in a positive manner will dramatically enhance our life.

Chapter 3

The Seven Stages of Life

———————

The Evolutionary Path of a Spirit in the Human Experience

According to the Group, the entire life process is broken down into seven separate stages. This information is important, they say, because it puts the human experience into a general timeline. Each stage of life has an overall purpose in the evolution of a soul, and all seven stages enable specific aspects of the twelve primary life lessons.

Stage One:

THE PLANNING STAGE
Prior to Birth

The first stage of life actually occurs prior to birth. This is when we plan the life we are about to experience. (This stage of life is discussed in greater detail in the chapter The Nature of Contracts.) It is during this stage that we ask certain people to play various roles in our life in order to help us with the specific life lesson we have chosen to work on this time around.

This stage is rarely remembered once we are in human form, even with hypnosis or other regression techniques. The reason for this is that if we did not have a 'veil of forgetfulness' in place, the game of life we come here to play would have very little meaning.

Gathering Spiritual Family

The first time we incarnated as humans, we came in with a group of souls that we knew well and trusted implicitly. This group is our original spiritual family. Over a period of subsequent lifetimes, we completed some of our contracts and discharged the karma we had built up with various members of our family. Being complete, we go on to form other extended spiritual families with other soul groups. Over the eons, we have all had many spiritual families with whom we have shared many lifetimes in many different combinations of relationships. Should we incarnate on opposite sides of the globe, we will invariably find one another when the time is right to activate a specific contract.

Even if some members of our spiritual family should already be incarnate on earth when we hold our 'pre-birth' planning meeting, they can still join us in spirit. Once gathered together, we will focus on choosing the primary life lesson around which all other contracts are based.

In the past, it was fairly easy to choose our life lessons, since it would often take as many as one hundred lifetimes to complete each one. In most cases, all that was needed was for us to set up new contracts for our next life that would best provide us with the necessary opportunities to master some of the attributes we would be working on. In those days, we would also have needed to take account of any karmic bonds and debts that we would have had with various members of our spiritual family.

It is at this stage that we also choose a male or female body. Unless there is a specific reason for us to choose a different gender, we often incarnate in the same gender we had in our previous lifetime. There are times, however, when the life lesson itself will dictate the gender we choose. This is because there are certain life lessons that are more easily mastered in one or the other gender. (This topic is covered in greater depth in the sections relating to these life lessons.)

Stage Two:

FIRST TRANSITION
Conception through the First Year

The Final Decision

The most difficult transition we make is the journey we take
through the birth canal. This is much more difficult than
the transition we call death, because the only way we can
make our transition from infinite form into the finite form of
a physical body is by lowering our level of vibration.

Both prior to and during the pregnancy process, we have
more opportunities to review all the potential connections
we have set up, and make our final decisions. In some
cases we may see that certain plans are no longer viable.
Since we always have free will, it's always possible for
other members of our spiritual family to take a direction
that makes it no longer possible for them to fulfill their
contracts with us. In this case, we might choose to bail
out and wait for a more appropriate time. This is the
reason behind many miscarriages. Many times in private
sessions, I have been able to help people connect to a
child they lost through miscarriage. The same also applies
in the case of some terminations. The only difference in
this instance is that the choice to terminate is made by
the mother (or both prospective parents), rather than the
incoming soul. The unfortunate thing about this is that
the decision to terminate is usually accompanied by what I
personally consider to be the most useless and destructive
human emotion of all – guilt. There are two important
things to bear in mind here. First, it simply is *not* possible
to kill a soul. Second, since this is the planet of free
choice, all of our choices are honored.

Assuming that all appears to be in order, and that both mother and child are still in agreement, the conception process begins. The first transition of a soul into physical form is accomplished in the womb. During the pregnancy the soul experiences its first human experience. Contrary to what many people think, communication between mother and fetus is often very strong. Sometimes in private sessions I have picked up on life-changing events that occurred when a client was in the womb. I've even had cases where I've discovered that a person is carrying the energy stamp (See the chapter on 'Energy Stamps - Energy Matrix') that had the effect of having been physically abused without ever having had the experience of such. In some cases these energy stamps have been transmitted as an energy stamp transfer from one of their parents or other influential people in their early life. This can be confusing to both client and facilitator, as it appears as if the experience of abuse happened to them, when in fact it may have only been transferred to them. Energy stamps that are transferred in this stage of life are very deeply rooted.

The Search for GOD

Even after birth, it is still possible for a soul to change its mind. This is often what happens in cases of infant death syndrome. Once again, however, it is important to remember that there is no blame or guilt attached to this decision; it is simply a matter of choice. Assuming we decide to remain, the first thing we do is to bond energetically with our parents or guardians, then with other family members and any important people in our immediate environment.

As soon as these connections are made, the search for higher meaning begins. This is also the time that we begin to absorb our first ideas about God. Most of us grow up believing that God is some omnipresent being that watches over us from above and takes care of our every need. The Group says that because our parents tower over us and we rely on them to fulfill our every need, we base our first impression of God on them. This is also why we believe that God and Heaven are always somewhere 'out there' and above us.

THE ENERGY ROLE MODEL

From virtually the moment we incarnate, we are primed to search for an energy role model. This will often be an adult within our vicinity who appears to have a similar energetic blueprint to us and upon whom we can model ourselves. This is usually done by contract and, in most cases, we choose someone other than our parents, often an aunt or uncle.

This contract, which can last throughout our entire lives, gives us confidence in our ability to cope with being in human form, as well as an energetic blueprint which becomes our guideline. Although it is most often an aunt, uncle or friend of the family, it can also be someone with whom we only have momentary contact. Such is often the case when we experience a brief, but deep and meaningful eye contact with a baby in some public place. Even though we may never see that child again, it will have received through the eyes the energetic imprint it was seeking, and in that moment we will have completed an important contract that we made with them. This is why focusing and making eye contact is so important for infants.*

---

*In the event of a blind child, most often these connections are simply delayed slightly while the child gets accustomed to carrying around a physical body and making these connections other ways.

Many times in private sessions I have encountered clients who never managed to connect with their energy role models. Although this is unusual, it can be intentional to facilitate a primary life lesson such as Acceptance, Truth or Trust. In these instances, I have found that these clients are usually lacking an inner sense of self. It's almost as if they feel as though they are a stranger in a strange land, playing the role of observer rather than participant.

Stage Three:

FIRST POWER
Age Two through Early Teen Years

As we become more accustomed to the human experience, we begin to remember that we are actually in control. It is at this point that we begin to start exercising our power. It is important for us to get comfortable with our own power at this stage of life for here we form imprints about personal power that we often carry for life. This is also known in child-rearing circles as the "terrible twos." The cries that once indicated need now invariably become an exercise in power. This is not the best time to teach a child responsibility, but neither is it appropriate to give in to every expression of a child's new-found power. Still, a child's growth and the way its expressions of power are accepted will have far-reaching effects on its life path.

The First Energy Stamps

Energy stamps are energetic imprints that are stamped upon us through experience. Their purpose is to facilitate the primary life lesson we are working on.*

---

*These are covered in greater detail in the chapter Energy Matrix – Energy Stamps.

Although energy stamps can be received at any time from the womb through early adulthood, the first time they strongly impact us is generally in the third stage of life. Energy stamps help set up the potential for us to focus our entire life path on the primary life lesson we have chosen. The most effective energy stamps are those that are directly related to our first expressions of personal power.

First Relationship Reflection

This is also a time when we begin to learn about balancing our power with those around us. While we may believe that we are omnipotent, this is the age at which we usually discover that others also believe the same thing. Thus, it is only when we start to form our own relationships that we begin to see the effect our use of power – as well as overuse of it – can have on other people. Because the first experience of anything is the most profound experience, these early relationships provide us with our first impressions about ourselves. This is why they often stay with us forever. This is also why most traditional therapies tend to focus specifically on what we experienced at this stage of life.

It is important to note that these energy stamps may be positive or negative. A positive example might be having parents who love and support us unconditionally. In this instance, we experience an acceptance of our first expression of power. Examples of negative energy stamps include emotional, physical and sexual abuse. Here, our power is not only rejected, but forcefully overridden, in which case we usually learn that is dangerous for us to express our power.

Failure to Express Power

Should we fail to express our personal power at this important stage, it is likely that we will learn to turn our rcreative energy (personal power) inward. This misdirection of energy can actually result in activating energy disorders such as depression, anxiety or other painful emotional conditions. Although there is mounting evidence that depression does not have genetic origins, it often follows an energetic line within family or close friends. Failure to express power in this stage of life can open the door to these and other potential energy challenges that may be in that energetic line.

Additionally, failure to express, and become comfortable with expressing power at this stage of life, can create a vacuum that often shows up in later adult life in more destructive ways. This vacuum is often a quiet yearning to express complete power over another. This can be filled in a variety of ways, including anger, manipulative behavior, bullying or any other way of forcing power on another person. Perpetrators of violent crimes, physical, mental and sexual abuse, pedophiles and more are often acting out of a misunderstanding of personal power that was not clearly defined at this stage of life. This is also the reason that we sometimes see seemingly normal people snap and become extremely violent. It is easy to see here that a person who feels repressed or robbed of the opportunity to express their personal power by being abused themselves will most likely repeat similar patterns as they grow into adulthood.

Adjusting our thoughts about children in this stage of life, and finding ways to help them become comfortable with expressing their own power, offers the greatest potential for human evolution in the years ahead.

Stage Four:

RESPONSIBILITY AND FIRST MATURITY
Late Teens through Late 30s

The Seeker

The fourth stage of life is when we, as souls in physical form, begin to take and express our power through making more mature decisions that will actually direct our lives. This is when we often use rebellion as a way to impose our newly-felt power. This second wave of power often leads us to feel invincible. This over-confidence in our power gives us the ideal situation in which to explore our boundaries. At this stage nothing is sacred, and we are constantly re-evaluating everything within our field. Even strong beliefs passed down from parents and teachers will be fearlessly examined in the new power of first maturity. This explains why we are often so changeable as teenagers and young adults.

Once we make it through the first three stages of life, we will have developed a more mature foundation for our power base, and a more realistic perspective about who we are.

Responsibility

At this stage we all have the opportunity to learn that personal responsibility is the balance to personal power. The Group offers the following suggestion: *Finding ways of increasing personal responsibility is the most effective way of increasing our personal power.* Although responsibility is not a primary life lessons in itself, it is an important component of several primary life lessons that relate to taking and exercising our own power.

Primary Life Lessons

If we have not yet embarked on the process of mastering our primary life lessons, the fourth stage of life is when this will often begin. What usually happens is that our catalyst will interact with us in a manner that is designed to activate our primary life lesson in either a positive or a negative manner. If we have chosen to facilitate our life lesson with an energy matrix, this is when it will become evident. This is when we usually home in on the direction in which we are going. This may not always be positive. For example, if we have already had several unsuccessful incarnations trying to master this life lesson through positive means, we will often turn to negative means to accomplish our goals, since we can often learn more from negative situations than we do from positive ones. This is not right or wrong, it's just human nature.

Second Level Relationships

Second level relationships usually develop at this point in our timeline. These usually comprise intense love interests and extremely close friendships that are likely to last a lifetime. This is when we begin to learn about the importance of balancing personal responsibility with power. This is when we begin to discover the joy and pleasure we can experience when we focus our efforts on making other people feel good about themselves.

Stage Five:

MATURITY
40s through 70s

The Enlightened Seeker

This is the stage of life when we begin to discover what is really important. We become enlightened seekers, striving always to express our passion and operating from our hearts. This is when what we *feel* becomes more important than what we *think*. It is when many of us experience a spiritual epiphany or awakening, and begin to re-evaluate everything we thought we knew. The interesting part is that when we later look back on this point in our lives, we generally recognize that all of our prior experiences were leading us to precisely this point. This is what some people refer to as seeing 'the big picture', or, all the pieces of the puzzle falling into place.

Redefining Self and Relationships

Having survived the strenuous experiences of raising children and creating a family life, this is when our focus turns towards self. This is when our own passion and joy begin to assume greater importance. Those who feel they have just been 'going through the motions' will often find themselves virtually exploding into other areas and interests in an attempt to find their passion and the true essence and meaning of their life. Many people tend to dismiss this as simply a 'mid life crisis' or 'empty nest syndrome,' or an over-reaction to the thought of becoming old. In fact, there is a lot more to this than merely trying to recreate one's youth. Attending to our own happiness at this stage is far more than merely self-indulgence; it is actually critical to our development as a soul. I see this as a very important second wake-up call. If you have not awakened by this time, the higher self will ensure that something will happen internally or externally to activate your awakening. This is often accomplished through a 'bump contract.'

Bump Contracts

Bump contracts can activate at this stage of life and can easily take the form of a brief romantic relationship. (These are covered in greater detail in the chapter 'The Nature of Contracts') What happens here is, if you are not on your chosen path, someone will come along, by contract, with such force that they will literally 'bump' you out of your rut and directly onto your path. Bump contracts are designed to work in both directions changing both participants' lives in a dramatic and sometimes very uncomfortable manner. Like all contracts, these are options that exist to accomplish a specific task and are completely governed by free choice.

Second Stage Life Lesson Activation

Even if we don't have a bump contract set up with someone, this will often be the time when our life lesson is reactivated and brought to our attention. If we have already been working on mastering our life lesson, there will be no need for any form of reactivation. But if we have chosen to bury our heads in the sand, you can bet that our life lesson will surface with a vengeance at this time. Unresolved issues will crop up in such a way that they will prove impossible to ignore.

Stage Six:

SIMPLIFICATION:
BECOMING LIKE A CHILD
The Conclusion of our Life in Physical Form

At this stage something usually happens that is designed to help us discern what is truly important. This is when we begin, usually on an unconscious soul level, to identify what is really important. After having gone through our re-evaluation period we start to simplify our lives. The Group refers to this period of life as becoming childlike. If we are to reenter Heaven and return Home, we need to start letting go of all the things that hold us on the earth plane. This includes people, possessions, and all earthly attachments. The only way we can achieve this is through becoming more like a child. In fact I believe the following reference from the New Testament corroborates this:

Matthew 18:3-4
"And He said: 'I tell you the truth, unless you change and become like little children, you will never enter the kingdom of heaven. Therefore, whoever humbles himself like this child is the greatest in the kingdom of heaven'."

The seventh and last stage of acclimation cannot be effectively accomplished until all our life experiences have been reduced to their core essence.

Being Pushed: "Dancing on Both Sides of the Veil"

Many of us fear becoming dependent on our children as we age. In fact, getting older is to be celebrated, not dreaded. One way to prevent our fears from materializing is to embrace the aging process. Those of us who avoid the simplification process will often be forced to experience this as a result of physical or mental debilitation.

Alzheimer's and other forms of dementia are very effective in helping us to accomplish the process of becoming childlike. Those who resist returning to the purity and simplicity of the childlike state will experience what it is like to dance on both sides of the veil simultaneously. While communicating physically in such cases can have its challenges, communication with the soul on a spirit level, as if the person had already died, can actually be very effective. Not only can communicating in this manner ease the person's confusion and frustration; it can even be used to give them permission to leave.

The Second Transition and Final Contracts

Although the second transition is what we call death, it is not the end of the seven stages of life. Death can either be very challenging, or a beautiful process, as well as a final gift for all involved. If those involved truly understand the process they will accept the gift with grace and ease. If not, they will have difficulty letting go.

If all parties are in agreement, this is where the final contracts take place. One important contract that will have been set up prior is with the person who has been chosen to give us permission to leave. This can be as simple as a son or daughter saying, "Dad, it's okay. You can go now. We love you. Don't worry, we'll take good care of Mom."

It's astonishing how many people nearing the end of life who have shown absolutely no interest in spirituality whatsoever, will suddenly become incredibly spiritual as they sense the end approaching. Regardless of what we believe, in the final analysis, we all return to spirit.

Another of our final contracts is that which we make with

the person who is going to be our 'greeter.' This is usually someone who knew us well enough to extend a hand from the other side and welcome us home.

Stage Seven:

ASSIMILATION
Incorporating life experiences into our core personality

Grounding

If we make a complete transition after we leave our body behind, we usually visit one or more of our loved ones on the earth plane.

Since we have only just left our body, it is easy to become confused and not recognize what has occurred. Our first thoughts are generally of a loved one. This almost instantaneously places us back into their field. Many times, all that is required is for us to say our goodbyes before we move on. Sometimes this will be a visual occurrence for the person left behind. At other times it may take place within a dream.

Re-membering Life

This final stage encompasses a review of all our life experiences and choices, as well as the effects of all our actions. This stage has often been referred to as the 'life review,' 'judgment day,' 'purgatory,' and a host of other descriptions. I think it's much simpler than this.

When we initially return Home, we go through an acclimation process. This is covered in greater detail in my book, *Re-member ~ A Handbook for Human Evolution,* in the chapter on HOME, where the Group referred to it as "Stretching out in Heaven." Once we have acclimatized to the energy there, we begin to meet other souls with whom we shared experiences while in physical form. Here we discuss what happened and how our contracts played out. Since there is no polarity on the other side, *all* life experiences – even pain – are re-membered as joyous.

Assimilating Life Experiences into the Core Personality

As we revisit and review each experience, we decide which experiences we will incorporate into our core personality and which will be released. There are times when we may choose to hold on to a negative experience and revisit it in a future lifetime. Such experiences are called energy stamps. (See the chapter Energy Stamps - Energy Matrix.) Since most energy stamps are used to facilitate mastery of a primary life lesson, we usually release them at this time. If we have yet to master the life lesson, we will set up new energy stamps in the next incarnation.

TWO QUESTIONS

During our experience of meeting friends and other souls that played an important part in our life experience, we are greeted with two questions. These are the only yardsticks against which most life experiences are measured. Once we comprehend these questions it is easier to see what is most important about life. They are simply:

Did you Dance in your Passion?
Did you Play in your Joy?

---

* It is possible for a soul to get confused and become earthbound.

Chapter 4

The Nature of Contracts

_____

The Building Blocks of Life

In our experience of life on Earth we mostly see things from a very limited perspective. Because of this, it's often very difficult for us to stop and shift our perspective when things start to go wrong. Often, we get so hung up on trying to figure out *what* we did wrong, that we never stop to consider that what we may be viewing as a disaster is, in fact, exactly the right and most appropriate thing that could be happening at that particular moment. The job we just lost, the marriage that just broke up, even the partner we may have just lost to a dreadful disease or accident… any one – and, in fact, *all* - of these events were part of our plan. They were set up to teach us an important lesson, to catapult us in a different direction, or even to jolt us awake and motivate us to find our passion.

These events, and many others, were part of the complex web of contracts, agreements and back-up plans we made in the scripting session prior to incarnating. We choose our lessons well in order to facilitate the life lessons we had decided we wanted to work upon so that we may learn the lessons that will fuel our advancement. . . If only we could just remember the script.

To understand the complete picture of the human experience from a spiritual perspective we must examine not only the events in life itself, but also those events that preceded our present life on earth.

When we look across a room at a party and see someone to whom we are intensely attracted we often don't know what to make of it. Our thoughts race round and round in an effort to find reasons for the attraction. If this leads to a relationship does this mean it was predestined? If so, what would have happened if we had decided not to go to the party that night? When such questions arise it is important to remember that there is really only one rule that we have set in place…

We always have free choice in all things

If we accept that free choice is the only real rule that we are to live by, then we must also understand that what we often view as predestination is, in fact, simply the result of a contract we have made. Since all contracts are contingent upon free choice, however, it can also be the case that we meet someone, recognize a deep connection and yet still choose to move in a different direction. The reality is that *all* contracts are only ever *potential* contracts until they are accepted by all parties involved.

Back-up Plans

We may decide to meet a person and enact a certain scenario that we contracted, and then pass one another by without stopping. We may even try to meet them again at a specific intersection further down the timeline. If our first plans don't come to fruition, and the contract is important to us as a soul, we will invariably arrange another opportunity in an entirely different setting much later on. For instance, a child who should have been our daughter may appear as a granddaughter instead, or if something prevents us from being born to the parents we chose, we may find our way into their family later on as the daughter-in-law with whom they feel a deep and exceptionally close bond. These are simply known as back-up plans, and I see them all the time in private sessions with people.

Once people know that their current situation is a back-up plan, they will often say something like: "I've always known that. I never felt like I belonged in my family, even though I love them. My sisters and brother all fit in and I don't. It's more than just being the black sheep of the family; they are just in a different world than I am."

When people know why they feel the way they do, the

knowledge can be life changing. It removes the pressure on them to conform to a particular family pattern, or to try to live up to the expectations their parents or siblings have for them. And even though it explains the reason why they have always felt different, it still leaves the responsibility for their own happiness with the individual, where it belongs. It is critical for all facilitators working with empowerment techniques to remember this at all times.

The problem is when we do finally adjust to the idea of contracts, we often tend to swing completely to the other side and give our power away to this concept and forget about free choice.

One of the hardest things for people to grasp is that not *all* events happen because of contracts. On the planet of free choice there is always *predisposition* but there is no *predetermination*. At the same time, however, it has to be said that few things occur by accident, as our higher selves are always orchestrating experiences to assist us in learning to master our life lessons. How we react to and deal with those experiences is entirely up to us. This is free choice in action.

Soul Mates

The concept of soul mates provides a perfect illustration of free choice in action. Actually the Group does not verify the 'one person for everyone' theory. While this is a very romantic ideal, it is not really practical for a free choice planet. The reality is that there are many possibilities for each of us. There are many back-up plans that we make for relationships, and most of them have to do with our primary life lesson. When I explain this to people many ask: "But what would happen if we should miss them all?" Actually, one of the greatest loves of all is the one that is built without any contracts in place. When this happens, the applause from the other side of the veil is deafening.

Although meeting a past love can be very powerful and romantic, the truth is every relationship must be rebuilt on a daily basis in order to last. Therefore, free choice, and the responsibility that goes along with it, play a much bigger role in all our relationships than most people realize.

Lineage Intent

When we script our contracts with parents, family and other important people in our lives, one of the factors we often consider most carefully is that of 'lineage intent.' What this means is that many families, or lineages, come in with a specific focus or intent. For example, it may be that one family may produce a long line of doctors or healers, while another may have an accomplished musician or artist in every generation. The famous seer, Edgar Cayce, came from one such lineage. When I met his niece, Caroline Cayce, she told me that, growing up, she believed that everyone had the same powers she had, and that it wasn't until she entered public school that she realized her gifts were not at all common. Clearly, Caroline had intentionally placed herself in a family with this particular lineage intent.

The Energy Role Model

One very important contract that is usually included in the first stage of life is the contract to be an energy role model. As described in the chapter on the Seven Stages of Life, this is a contract that involves two people with a substantial age difference who cross each other's path at the perfect time to give the younger person an energetic blueprint to model him or herself on. This allows the awakening souls to see what they will be like as they grow. It is even possible to have a contract for an energy role model with a person you will never know but happen to pass on the street. The next time you see a young child staring intently at you for what seems like a very long time, consider that there may be a contract there and let them in to make contact with you. Both of you will benefit from it.

This usually shows up in my sessions when people have not managed to find their energy role models. When this happens, they often experience great difficulty getting a handle on their own sense of being. This can lead to the manifestation of many unwanted patterns, including several that can be misinterpreted as primary life lessons. This is why, when conducting private sessions, identifying whether the clients have a good sense of self is one of the first things I do, as this indicates to me that they have found their energy role model. If they have not, I gently explain the concept to them and share with them the reason why they probably feel so disconnected in many areas. Although it does not solve their problem, it does provide them with trust in their own inner feelings that something was missing.

Other Contracts

Transition Contracts - These are often one of the most important contracts we can make. This is the contract we make with an individual to release us when we are dying. Sometimes, if the relationship is very close, this person will actually be able to say the words: "It's okay to leave, Mom. You can let go if you like. We will all be fine." If this level of communication is not in place before we die, this same contract may be activated with more common superficial language like: "Mom, know that we are all with you to help make this easier." This may be all that it takes to activate the contract and give them permission to leave.

Greeters - These are people who agree to greet us in spirit when we transition home. Sometimes it's a husband or wife that has passed over ahead of us, but most of the time it's someone less close to us, like an aunt or uncle, or possibly a friend we knew in high school.

Transitioning to the other side is probably the second most difficult thing we will ever do in this life. Contracts that we make with those who will help us to transition are very important. The most difficult transition we make is the transition into this life via the birth process.

Bump Contracts – These are safe-guard contracts usually made in the first stage of life. These contracts always involve a person with whom we will have had a very close, intimate connection in at least one previous lifetime. This person agrees to intersect our life at a critical time in order to check that we are on the path we set out to travel. As souls we are aware that many times we get stuck in situations that can distract us from accomplishing our real work. These contracts are designed to come together with such intensity that they cannot help but jolt us out of our routine. Their purpose is to remind us of our original soul intention and direction. Quite often these appear as irresistibly romantic encounters. By their very nature they must be strong enough to 'bump' us into some kind of new awareness. Their very strength is often sufficient to tempt us into an affair in the mistaken belief that at last we have found our soul mate. It is helpful to bear in mind that although they can become successful long term relationships, they were originally intended to be short term only. Bump contracts always create an opportunity for both parties to change the direction of their lives.

Karmic Contracts

Karma, as we know it, has now been released to enable us to evolve more rapidly. During our planning sessions in the first stage of life, however, many karmic contracts are still being chosen. While this is not a necessity, it is simply that these may provide the most effective means to facilitate a primary life lesson, especially when we pick up a relationship that we left incomplete in a previous life. Since it is no longer possible to build a long-term relationship on the basis of karma, any new karmic contracts that we do choose to set up will need to be completed very quickly.

Minor Contracts and Non-contracts

Not all contracts are directly related to our primary life lessons. Many of our contracts have more to do with the other people involved than they have to do with us. Sometimes we are simply holding the space as players in someone else's contract. Although we have a tendency to take everything in life very personally, oftentimes it is really not about us, even though we may be involved in a situation to the extent that it appears as though it is happening *to* us. "Sometimes," as the Group is fond of reminding me, "a cup of coffee is just a cup of coffee."

Chapter 5

Night Games

When the Lights go Out

As the sun sets each day on our evolving planet, we enter into another dimension. This dimensional reality is one with which we are all familiar. We call it simply nighttime. The majority of this alternate reality is currently used for sleep and to rejuvenate our bodies on a daily basis. These rest times, and how we use them, are going to change and become even more important as we shift into a higher vibrational state. These changes are necessary to align us with the new capabilities many of us are developing. One of the primary changes we will experience as we evolve has to do with sleep.

The "3:00 a.m. Club"

If you have been experiencing strange disruptions in your sleeping patterns, congratulations! Though you may not be aware of it, you are an elite member of what has come to be known by many as the 3:00 a.m. club, so called because this is the time at which many people are now finding themselves awaking. If you thought you were the only one experiencing this, be assured you are not alone. We first started noticing it about five years ago. Now, whenever we ask for a show of hands at our seminars, around eighty percent of our attendees generally respond. This is nothing to be alarmed about; it merely indicates that your personal evolution has begun. These and other changes will occur in your sleeping patterns as you advance your spiritual development.

The Triad of Sleep

Many people experiencing this phenomenon are often troubled by it. They worry about not being able to sleep through the night and then being tired the following day. In fact, not only is this quite normal; it's going to become even more commonplace in the future. Mankind is simply developing a new sleeping pattern, which I refer to as the 'triad of sleep.' I call it this because what happens is that you sleep for approximately three hours, wake for two, and then sleep again for three. These two hours or so in the middle of the night will soon become a joyfully anticipated wakeful rejuvenation period. In fact, this new sleeping pattern is already much more prevalent than you may know.

Taking short naps during the day will also become commonplace. These 'rejuvenation naps' will be strategically timed to inspire your spirit as well as to rest your physical body. Besides making a difference in the way your body physically deals with energy, this new sleeping pattern is also designed to allow your body to rejuvenate itself during the daytime, as well as the nighttime.

As our physical bodies start adapting to these new sleeping patterns, we will find ourselves spending approximately one twelfth of our day in a *wakeful rejuvenation* period. This period will generally occur in the special two-hour time frame that commences when we awake at 3:00 a.m. 3:00 a.m. club members span all age and socio-economic groups and generally have started this process only in the last five years. Most also began the process by waking up and glancing at the clock at *exactly* 3:00 a.m.

One could argue that this is nothing more than a natural physiological process, which science would explain by saying that this is the period during our normal sleep cycle when the body reaches its highest temperature. Biologists will tell you that this is true. Still, it doesn't explain why the number of people experiencing this phenomenon has increased so dramatically over the past five years. I consider this to be just one more piece of evidence that humankind is evolving at an astounding rate.

More importantly, however, it's important to understand that during this wakeful period we are in a state of enhanced creation. We know from studies of the brain that when we are in an 'alpha state,' we're actually in an enhanced state of awareness.

There are four brainwave frequency patterns: *Beta, Alpha, Theta and Delta.* Our brains produce all four frequencies simultaneously. However, at any given time one frequency is more dominant. The alpha state is the pattern that our brains produce naturally when we are very relaxed, i.e., just prior to falling asleep, or when we are particularly engrossed in something such as a chore or hobby, or when we are glued to the TV or a movie. To an onlooker, it may appear as if we are in a daze or a trance, when, in fact, we are in an enhanced state of awareness that allows us to be *more* aware of everything that is going on around us. Hypnosis has utilized the alpha state to access and program what is commonly known as the subconscious mind, or, as others prefer to regard it, tapping into the Universal Energy that binds us all together.

Imagine that energy flows through everything and everyone, permeating all things. We know from science that when all energies are removed from a predefined space and a perfect vacuum is formed, there is still a measurable energy that exists within that space. This is the Universal Energy. We are all an integral part of this flow, as this is the energy that ties us all together as one.

As we evolve as humans and our awareness expands, we will see a natural movement toward unity consciousness. As we do, everything that connects us with the Universal Energy will become better understood and less mystical. Placing our brains in an alpha state is one way we can enhance this connection.

When we awaken in the middle of the night, we're not only

in an enhanced awareness, we're also in an enhanced state of creation. In this state, our ability to transform our thoughts into reality is greatly increased. The challenge is to become conscious of what we are thinking about and, therefore, what we are creating. The problem is that most people fail to use these powers consciously. Instead, they simply allow their creations to flow through them by default, thereby creating realities that are not really to their liking.

For example, let's say that Tom awakens at 3:00 a.m. for the third night in a row. First, he is frustrated as he tries to figure out why he is waking up at 3:00 a.m. every night. Then he starts worrying about the important meeting that he has scheduled in the morning, afraid that he will be too tired to make an effective presentation. Instead of consciously using the enhanced state of creation to manifest something positive, he unknowingly manifests two unwanted creations. The first has to do with his frustration at awakening three nights in a row. Had Tom simply observed these occurrences, nothing would have happened. Instead, believing it to signify that something was wrong, he invested more energy into his 'problem' by worrying about what it might mean. In turn, he becomes even more anxious and concerned, which then created the perfect scenario for a self-fulfilling prophecy to awaken him every morning at exactly 3:00 a.m.

The second mistake Tom made was to create and transmit the thought that he would be extremely tired the next day, which would affect his important presentation. So guess what happened? Since Tom was in an enhanced state of creation these thoughts were not ones that simply came and went. Rather, they were sent out as enhanced creations, which then manifested into reality. The result was that Tom could hardly keep his eyes open during his presentation the following day. Worse yet, because he found it impossible to throw off his frustration at having been awake at 3:00 a.m. the night before, his continual fretting only succeeded in ensuring that he would once again awaken at 3:00 a.m. the following night. As most of us do, Tom blamed all manner of outside sources for controlling his reality, when in fact it was Tom himself who was the architect of his own predicament.

Like Tom, most of us are not generally very adept at monitoring or mastering our thoughts. With the evolution of humanity that is now unfolding, the time has come for us to start choosing our thoughts very carefully, for not only do they create our reality, but in the new energy they will do so with very little time lag.

Thus, if you should find yourself awakening and worrying about being tired the next day, you will create precisely what you are afraid of. By the same token, if you should find yourself awakening with a feeling of excitement at what this special time could bring, you will find yourself filled with enthusiasm and boundless energy the following day. Remember, you may not have control over what thoughts enter your mind but you *do* have complete control over what stays there. So choose your thoughts with great care.

Rather than tossing and turning and bemoaning your sleeplessness, why not view this time as a perfect opportunity to do something for yourself for your ultimate benefit. For example, you could read a book that lifts your spirits, entertain yourself in some other way, allow yourself to daydream about all the wonderful ambitions and plans you have for improving your life… or, you could try something really unusual and simply allow yourself to *be*.

Sex ~ A Tool for Rejuvenation

Since this is a period when your senses will be especially heightened, why not use this time to make love? After all, sexual expression is a perfect activity for rejuvenation as this time is made for engaging in creativity and experimentation. Plus, you never know... you may just create some wonderful experiences for yourself.

We all have different facets to our personality and character, some of which we are unaware of, and some of which we're too inhibited to display. This wakeful period is an ideal time to explore parts of ourselves that we never knew existed, or that we rarely allow out to play. You could have fun playing different roles that propel you beyond your normal boundaries. You may be surprised at what surfaces.

No matter what age or physical condition, sexual expression in some form is always possible. Since to rejuvenate means to make younger and revitalize, we would all be wise to not dismiss this expression of love as a form of rejuvenation, for it's far more important than we realize.

If you do not have a partner to play with, then consider using some of these techniques by yourself. Since all love is actually a reflection of self love, it's a really good place to start. Now is a very good time to start rethinking old, self-limiting belief systems. If you are having difficulty communicating with your partner, consider waking them the next time you find yourself awake at 3:00 a.m. and simply allow your bodies to communicate on their own level. They may thank you the next day.

The vibrations of Home are very strong. The Group says that we experience brief glimpses of Home in moments of passion, such as when we are making love. If you can imagine that our place of origin as a soul (whether you call that Home, Heaven or unity consciousness) has the same energy that we experience during our moments of sexual pleasure, you will see why I say that sex will become more important as we evolve as spiritual beings in human form. Many spiritual seekers see sex as an earthly desire and, thus, mistakenly assume that the more they grow spiritually, the more their desire for sex should diminish. On the contrary, the more we raise our vibrational level, the more likely we are to experience an increase in our desire for sexual expression. It could even be said that the experience of unconditional love through sex is preparation for living in the higher energy of our evolved state. This is because when we raise our vibrations, our energy centers, or chakras, spin faster. In addition to rejuvenating us physically, this also stimulates the basic sexual energy that is often refered to as Kundalini energy. Granted, this may prove somewhat challenging for those whose upbringing may have conditioned them to associate sex with guilt, rather than pleasure. But it's important to remember that sex is a perfectly natural human activity that also happens to rejuvenate the entire being, physically, emotionally and spiritually, and should be honored as a beautiful and very powerful expression of love. It is in this same understanding that some have even found spirituality through sexual expression. It's more than shouting "Oh God" at the appropriate moment; it's the basis of the ancient Hindu spiritual practice of Tantra that finds spiritual expression through the natural flow of sexual energy. From a spiritual standpoint "the Group" often reminds us that we have a magical attribute that they don't. We can touch one another.

Since we have had such difficulty claiming our powers of creation, we instinctively look to higher authorities in an attempt to resolve our confusion concerning sex. As we continue this evolutionary process, however, we will learn to listen to our own bodies for clues about which way to turn. We will learn to listen within, rather than go without. Guilt, shame and modesty concerning sex are deeply ingrained in our psyche as a result of misusing sex over eons. Throughout our entire history as a species of humans, sex has been used as a means of control in one form or another. This has left us with deep-seated scars that keep us from listening to our own bodies.

Deep within our cellular memories remain energy stamps that equate the sex act with weakness. The guilt we associate with sex has hampered our understanding of the true meaning of this expression of passion. Yet it's important to remember that in the new energy, the dissolution of guilt in relationships will be a necessary component in developing unconditional love. This allows us to experience passion on all levels including the physical. In order to progress in our evolution as humans, much healing will need to take place in this area.

Same Sex Relationships

As we evolve, we will develop a greater understanding of the true nature and purpose of sexual expression. The further we move toward unity consciousness, the more we will see a rise in same sex relationships. While this may shock some, here again, it is very important to understand that Love is the base energy from which all other energy is transmuted. *All* expressions of love are divine. Love is not a thing. . . it is an energy, and therefore only exists when it is circulating. To restrict that circulation in any manner will be like fighting against the tide of the ocean. There will be those who think that same sex relationships are a disorder that can be cured. And, yes, there will be those who see this as a threat to their own sense of security. Nevertheless, we cannot hold back evolution. Judgment of others or ourselves will only hold back the advancement of all. If the opposite of love is fear then it is easy to see how the increase in same sex relationships can easily trigger fear in many people. Humans throughout history have always been afraid of things they do not understand and, in fact, fear is only a lack of understanding. This area will be no exception, yet, it will be an excellent growth opportunity for many stuck in fear. Still, the truth is there's nothing to fear as all expressions of love lead to a higher understanding of love for all. All that's happening is that we, as a species, are beginning to experiment with expressions of love in unity consciousness.

Some may find greater expression of love where they never thought to look; others may never feel the need for such experiences. What's important is to find your own truth and make space for the truth of others. In the final analysis, it is all Love.

There are two ways in which people experience same sex attractions. One is through an 'Energy Stamp' and the other is as a result of their 'Energy Matrix'. An 'Energy Stamp' is acquired through experience. From an evolutionary perspective, this is actually determined on a soul level in the first stage of life, and often is directly related to the soul's primary life lesson. An 'Energy Matrix,' on the other hand, is simply the way one is wired for energy. (See the chapter Energy Matrix – Energy Stamps.) The increase we are now seeing in same sex relationships has nothing to do with energy stamps, but rather, is a result of the individuals concerned coming in already wired with this sexual orientation. In other words, it is their energy matrix.

At the same time, this does not mean that there will be a corresponding decrease in opposite sex relationships. In general there will be a rise in *all* areas of love relationships as we move into our next stage of evolution as humans. From an evolutionary perspective, expect also to see an increase in many forms of sexual expression and new forms of relationships that reflect unconditional love. This will confuse many people, since we are more accustomed to basing our relationships on conditional, as opposed to unconditional, love. As with all radical changes, patience and understanding, both with ourselves and others, during this shift will go a long way toward making this transition easier for all of us. Contrary to most spiritual teachers, I strongly believe that sex and love relationships in many forms will become more important to all of us in the near future as we move closer toward recreating Home on this side of the Veil.

Procreation ~ Conceiving Light

For those planning to become parents, this period provides a wonderful opportunity to take time together beforehand and invite the child's energy to connect with your own and communicate with you. Don't be concerned if you do not hear words or receive clear messages. Simply opening up a space to feel the child's energy allows him or her to play an active role in the process. And don't be afraid to share with your partner what you are feeling, or any information you are receiving. It is quite a feat for the soul of your child to get through to you when you are busy. There are literally times when you are looking at books of names, wondering what to select, with the spirit of the child who is about to enter whispering over your shoulder. Allowing this special quiet time together will enable the child to communicate with you more clearly.

Don't be surprised if the name it whispers sounds familiar; it's not uncommon for souls to incarnate many times with similar-sounding names.

Many in same sex relationships also may be choosing to parent. If this should apply to you, it can be very beneficial to invite the child's energy to join with yours before the physical union. Regardless of whether you are physically bearing a child, or adopting one, it always helps to take time to welcome the child's energy into the union. First create the bond in the ethereal, then seal the contract as you connect in the physical. This will open the way for an easy transition and acclimates everyone's energies to each other. This enables a strong energetic bond of love to form between parents and child ahead of time so that when the child arrives it will very quickly feel at home. This is a wonderful, loving way to give your child a head start in life.

Night Work

As we move forward, some may find that they have no difficulty sleeping but often wake up tired, as if they have been working all night long. It may surprise you to know that this is indeed the case. Telepathic energy connections are often made during sleep when one travels through inter-dimensional realities. Most often, what takes place is that as you travel in your sleep you encounter others in need of help. Being the healers that you are, you cannot pass up an opportunity to lend assistance.

The misdirection of energy comes when you begin to feed other beings energetically and they become dependent upon your energy. No one can tell you if this is happening; you will know it in your own heart. If you find this to be true, look for ways that you can center your own energy in your wakeful state. That will help you to set healthy boundaries in the inter-dimensional realm.

Dreams ~ Their Real Purpose

There are many different purposes and uses for our dream state. Those of you who have studied dream interpretation know that it is not possible to make definitive statements about the meaning of all dreams. Remember – we are spiritual beings having a physical experience, and thus only a very small portion of our true selves is housed within the bubble of biology we inhabit. When we sleep, our biology rejuvenates the energy field around it. The remainder of our energy, or higher self, which never rests, is always connected with the Universal Energy. Thus, dream time is a time for our higher self to set up energy fields for us to experience during wakefulness, and to speak to our lower, physical self, unhampered by our conscious thought processes.

Each soul uses dreams in different ways, and therein lies the challenge of defining a set of standards for interpreting our dreams.

All dreams to some extent provide a way of traveling into alternate realities. There are several things that can be accomplished through these journeys. The list below details a few of the dream types and their attributes.

Rejuvenation Dreams

These are dreams of the mind. Certain activities rejuvenate our minds and, therefore, our actual thought processes. These activities involve a constant stream of changes, often in the form of exceedingly imaginative dreams, whose purpose is to stimulate and challenge our human minds to adapt. If we re-member these dreams upon waking, our conscious mind will search our memory banks in an attempt to find real-life experiences to help assimilate the dream into our reality. If it can find such an experience, the dream will be assimilated and then quickly forgotten, as it will have served its purpose. In the rare event that you have no life experience to associate with it, such a dream will remain in your consciousness as a vivid memory which may then be manifested in some form or another in your daily life. These dreams not only have a profound effect upon our physical bodies, they also trigger the rejuvenation process.

Perspective Dreams

Perspective dreams consist of sleep experiences in which our higher self directs us on a journey that is designed to change our point of view or shift our perspective. All dreams are perspective dreams to some extent. Something happens in our dream that shifts us into an alternate reality, which then allows us to see and understand something from a new point of view. Perspective dreams are usually remembered in vivid detail. They are also accompanied by very strong emotions. Many times such dreams will be remembered for how we *felt*, rather than what they were actually about.

As with all dreams, they can be positive or negative experiences. It's important to keep in mind, however, that this is merely an illusion of polarity and, therefore, will not be seen in the same light when viewed by our higher self. It only becomes a good dream or a nightmare when we label it so with our conscious minds.

There are times when our higher self begins to position our physical self for a lesson that we may wish to experience. Sometimes our higher self introduces a vivid dream that easily shifts our perspective. Perhaps in it a loved one dies or a horrific tragedy occurs. While we may tend to view this as a "bad" dream, there's no denying it's very effective. Upon awakening from such an experience, it would certainly shift our perception of what is really important.

There are alternate realities that run concurrent to our own. There is another "you" that may be experiencing a slightly different set of circumstances caused by different choices that you may have made in another reality. This is now much more than conjecture, as is evidenced by recent articles in such magazines as *Discover*, *Scientific American* and other scientific publications which substantiate these same concepts as a direct implication of cosmological order, instead of science fiction.

From the article 'Alternate Realities' Scientific American, May 2003

According to the latest scientific observations, our known universe is 4 x 10^{26} meters in length, and scientists theorize that there is another 'you' in a parallel universe about 10 x 10^{28} meters from where you are reading this right now. This observation, which suggests that each universe is part of a larger 'multiverse,' actually quantifies many other scientific theories of empirical science, including the theory of relativity. What we will find as we continue our evolution is that we exist as a soul in each of these parallel universes simultaneously, and that during times of rejuvenation the soul connects with all the fragments of ourselves in all multiverses. This will most often show in the beginning stages of our awareness as dreams.

These dreams also provide a way of jumping between realities and viewing events in our current reality against a different backdrop. These are the types of dreams that many of us love to interpret. Here, we are actually seeing aspects of our lives in a different reality. In these dreams we may find characters that we feel we 'know,' even though in our 'real' life we don't know any such person. These dreams are among those that are often the most re-membered. By interpreting aspects of them we can bring to the forefront of our consciousness a message that our higher self has planted in our subconscious.

Prophetic Dreams
These are the result of a specific connection that occurs with our higher self in sleep state. In effect, they are the direct result of meeting ourselves in an alternate reality. This is a way for our higher self to plant seeds and communicate ideas to our physical self. They are akin to time travel in that we are meeting ourselves in the inter-dimensional levels of time and space. Were such an event to occur in a wakeful state, our consciousness would not have any reference for it.

However, the prophetic dream rarely unfolds in our normal reality exactly as it was envisioned in our dream. This is because the event has yet to take place in current reality, but in fact is an experience that has already happened in an alternate multiverse. Because the time line perspectives relate to completely different universes, the two realities rarely unfold identically.

This type of dream is the most prevalent at this time in our evolutionary history, and many of us are having such dreams every night. They are also the type of dream that is rarely recalled into our conscious memory. Their purpose is to warn us of what lies ahead so that we may be prepared for the choices that await us when we awaken. This is why we often get a feeling of 'knowingness' about something that is about to happen. These dreams also serve to unite our soul's experience in all alternate realties, and are the basis of what we call rejuvenation. In order to rejuvenate we must reunite the soul.

The important part to re-member with these dreams is that they are only accurate at the time they are received. *We always have choice in all matters.* Even though these prophetic dreams are rarely re-membered consciously, they imprint us with feelings about what lies ahead. Many people with strong psychic abilities actually tap into this energy by 'reading' the feelings that were imprinted during these dreams. Since we have choice at all times we can actually change the timeline of the events. Therefore, even the experience of vivid but largely un-remembered nightmares may shift the outcome of the experience itself.

There are times when we may experience an inner knowing about which way to turn, but have no idea why or how we know this. What's happening here is that our higher self is planting seeds for the future. That said, it is important always to remember that, since nothing is predestined, things still may not materialize as they appeared in the dream. Our reality is always a result of our choices. For this reason, all dreams are not only prospective, but also prophetic to some degree.

Emotionally Prophetic Dreams

These are the most wondrous dreams that usually plant seeds through an emotional experience. We may be able to recount these dreams in intimate detail, yet even as we replay the dream we may find it being enhanced. For instance, we may be able to remember a dream and tell someone about a man who was driving a car in it. Then, as we're saying the words we may become aware that we know much more about this man than was evident in our dream. We may somehow know that he is a habitual liar and not to be trusted. Or that he was sad, or had just experienced a loss. We may envision an image of his wife even though we cannot explain where in the dream we learned this. And while the details of such dreams may fade soon after awakening, the feelings associated with them may remain just as strong for several days.

The seeds planted by our own higher self during such dreams will sprout and emerge to prepare us for an emotional experience that will take place in the near future. The interesting part about these dreams is that while we may remember them in such great detail that we will often feel compelled to tell someone or write them down, the moment we do ground the energy in this manner we will begin to lose the feeling.

Energy Balancing Dreams

Energy balancing dreams have a specific purpose in that they provide us with a way to balance our energy fields. They generally are not meant to be remembered upon waking. Sometimes when we've had a bad day, we may have absolutely wonderful dreams at night to help balance our energy. Conversely, sometimes when we've had a day filled with beautiful heart connections and love, our

Higher Selves will balance our energy with what seems like a negative dream. If we should bring these dreams into consciousness they will generally be extremely intense and vivid. The biggest challenge is that when we do experience dreams of such intensity, we naturally look for a deeper meaning. It's helpful to remember that sometimes the obvious is all that there is. Giving power to a dream that was never meant to be remembered can actually result in creating a reality out of a vision whose only purpose was to balance our energy through brief exposure.

Self-Directed Dreams
As we progress, dreams will become a way in which we can learn intentionally to jump between alternate realities. The art of Be-ing is the same as Be-ing aware. There is a direct connection to our well Be-ing and our ability to simply *be*. Lucid dreaming – i.e., becoming aware that we are having a dream while we are still in it – is one of the first steps toward Be-ing. Our consciousness is capable of extending far beyond our energy field. Becoming accustomed to intentionally extending our energy fields through the use of self-directed dreams will help prepare us for many of the wonders that lie ahead as we evolve.

When the Lights Go Down

Night is a magical time, a special time for balancing and refreshing our energy fields. Sleep, and the way we use it, is one area that is changing very quickly. The energy of night is the dark side of Light. In the days when magic was prevalent on the Earth, it was most often performed at night.

Here's an example of an energy-balancing dream. I have known my wife and partner, Barbara, since high school and she has always been a vivid dreamer. She often wakes in the morning with all the excitement of a child on Christmas day and recounts to me the most detailed dreams. There was a time, however, when she realized that she seemed to have stopped dreaming. We had just finished a seminar and were still spinning from all the excitement. If you have never been to one of the Lightworker seminars, the best way I can describe them is to say that for two days you are 'Home.' Connecting with true family, you stretch your heart chakra as far as it will go, and then find ways to stretch it even more. Since we do these seminars every two weeks you might think that we would have become so accustomed to them that they would no longer affect us in the same way. That's not the case. For us, each one is as powerful an experience as the very first gathering.

After one seminar, as we retired for the night Barbara asked to remember her dreams. The next morning she was very difficult to awaken. When I finally woke her she was in a very pensive mood. Eventually she told me that she'd dreamed that one of our sons had died in a motorcycle accident. She was really shaken. Since we were in Europe there was a delay before we could call home. That day was very difficult for her, but when we got through on the phone both boys were fine. It was only after she had taken her first deep breath of the day that our youngest son, Brent, told her that he'd had a minor crash on his motorcycle. He was fine, it was Barbara that was a nervous wreck.

Since she had remembered the dream, Barbara looked to interpret the experience. She asked me if I could tell her what that had all been about. She has always been very connected to our boys and usually knows intuitively what is happening with them at all times. She could not understand why she'd had the dream or why she was shaken so badly by it.

The Group explained that because Barbara had been so high on energy for so long, it had actually put her out of balance. This dream had been her higher self's way of bringing her energy back into balance. She was not originally intended to remember the dream, but since she had asked to re-member *all* her dreams the Universe responded with . . . *and so it is.*

When Barbara wants to remember dreams now she asks to remember *only* those dreams that will make her feel good.

Chapter 6

Clearing the Energy Tubes

Connecting to the Earth through Emotions

The human experience is geared toward seeking. Whether we seek to make more money, enhance our life style, improve our health or relationships, or strive for spiritual enlightenment, we all share the impulse to improve on what we have or who we are. This is what we refer to when we talk about being on a 'path.' In fact, it is the desire 'to be on our paths' (whatever that path may be) that motivates us in most areas of our lives. (It is interesting to note, however, that this 'path' we talk about never seems to have an end.) Thus, just like energy itself, we humans are always in motion.

Most of us believe that our paths are mapped out for us, and to a degree, they are, since we do come in with certain contracts to fulfill. This is not to suggest that we are puppets, dancing to the tune of some higher power. On the contrary, we are the creators and thus we always have free will. According to the Group, we are creating our own experience in every moment. The only way we can actually find and be on our path is to create it, which, of course, we are doing all the time. In fact, this act of creation not only brings us back to our point of origin, but is also the reason we are here. Basically, we are the creator searching for something to create.

So, how do we create?

Imagine that you have an energy tube that runs from the top of your head, down through the length of your body, ending just beneath your feet. Now, what if I told you that your highest purpose on this Earth is to take ethereal items and run them through that tube in order to bring them down to earth and give them substance? Would this not be the perfect definition of creation?

Fig 1

Picture Caption: Energy Tubes. The collector on top represents our connection to our higher self. This is now growing much larger and is drawing more energy through our tubes, which in turn stretch to accommodate the increased energy.

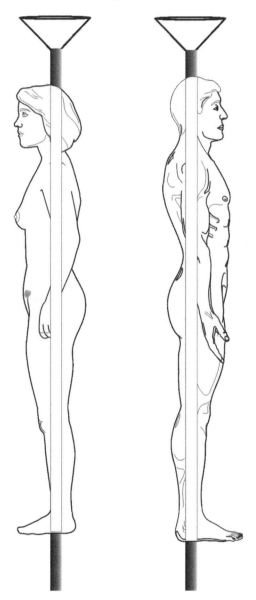

Ethereal items are objects that have no mass in this universe; whereas the Earth, is entirely mass and substance. We all have these tubes and we use them every day to bring the ethereal into our world and give it form. A simple way to describe this process: *Everything that is man-made first began its life as an ethereal thought form.* Turning something ethereal, such as a concept, an idea or a thought form, into something that has mass and substance in our world can only be accomplished by using an energetic creation tube. Since this tube would bridge the gap between the ethereal and physical world, such a tube could be neither completely physical, nor completely ethereal in nature. Since energy does have mass, however, and yet at the same time is not completely physical, it provides the perfect material to compose these tubes.

The concept of energy tubes that run the length of the body in front of the spinal column and into the earth was given to me as a visual image to explain some very important points about how we create our lives. As long as we are using our ability to create through these energy tubes, we move forward on our life path. In essence, all moves smoothly. It is only when we believe that we cannot create or that we are restricted in some way that we experience difficulties.

In order to understand the characteristics of energy tubes we must first look at the process of how we actually use them.

We think of love as an *emotion*, but I'd like to suggest that love is actually *energy*. It only exists when it is moving from one form to the other. For instance, we know that the only way to have love in our lives is to give it away freely, for it is only when we give love away that it can circulate and return. In fact, I would even go so far as to suggest that love is the base energy from which *all* other energies are formed. Songs often tell such truths in words like, "love is all there is." Moreover, as we move further into the new energy of our evolution it will *only* be possible to create with the base energy of love.

We are so much more than our physical bodies. The Group suggests that the largest part of our selves is contained outside of our physical being. We often refer to this as our higher selves. Many people do not feel they are in touch with their higher selves in any way. Yet as we progress and move forward in our evolution, our connection to our higher selves is growing stronger every single day. The basis of all our higher senses, including intuition, is found in the connection to our *higher self.*

Thirty or forty years ago, the buzzword for this higher sense was *ESP.* It was something that everyone was talking about. If people had strange powers or showed any psychic ability, they were regarded as having *Extra Sensory Perception,* or *ESP.* Today, we know there's nothing extraordinary or magical about ESP. In fact, it's so common, we don't need fancy words to describe it. We all have experiences of 'knowing' things without knowing how we know them. We simply refer to this as our basic human intuition. This is an example of how our connection to our higher self is becoming stronger in the new energy.

There are two ways that our higher selves interact with our physical, or lower, selves. One is by inhabiting an energy vehicle known as the energy matrix. An energy matrix and its characteristics are chosen in the planning stages of life prior to birth. These are our energy bodies. The energy matrix is the way in which we are wired and it controls the ways in which we experience life.

Your energy matrix not only determines how you first deal with energy as it enters your field; it also facilitates any primary life lessons you may be working on during your present incarnation. Once an energy matrix is chosen, it stays with you throughout your entire lifetime (and future lifetimes) until it is mastered. An energy matrix cannot be healed, as nothing is actually wrong; it can only be mastered.

The other way in which we facilitate life lessons is through energy stamps. Energy stamps are imprinted upon us as a result of specific events, circumstances or incidences that occur (usually during childhood) in our present lifetime. These experiences 'stamp' us with a specific energy pattern that causes us to behave or respond in a particular manner over and over again, until something happens to change that behavior pattern. Unlike an energy matrix, however, energy stamps don't have to stay with us throughout our lifetime, since they can be healed or replaced with more productive or appropriate behaviors and response patterns.

Overcoming an energy stamp is a huge accomplishment and is a perfect example of true empowerment. This goes far beyond what we regard as self-empowerment, because of the way that the properties of energy stamps relate to time. Because an energy matrix is part of our *infinite* self, it is not related to the human experience of time, which is why we can never heal it, only master it. Because an energy stamp is firmly rooted in the timeline of our *finite* selves, when we change it, it is altered backwards and forwards on our timeline.

When we heal an energy stamp within ourselves, we tap into the timeline of our present reality and alter it. Since linear time (past, present and future) is only an illusion of the polarity in which we live, we can actually heal the 'sins of our fathers' as well as those of our children. This is why healing our energy stamps is no small accomplishment, because we are actually making far more of a difference than we may ever know.

This also explains why it is not uncommon for people who work on forgiving someone for past abuses to find that the person they forgive has underjgone a subtle personality change. We may believe they have changed purely because we forgave them, but in reality it has more to do with the healing of an energy stamp that has far-reaching effects in both our timelines. If the energy stamp involved someone who played the role of catalyst in a primary life lesson we are working with, the changes in our relationship with that individual are often quite dramatic as we actually change our contract with that person. What basically happens is that by healing the energy stamp, we effectively free the other person from having to play the role they agreed to undertake to help us master our life lesson, which of course changed the entire nature of the relationship we had with them.

In understanding the timeline concept, it is helpful to keep in mind that we live with the illusion of being separate from one another when, in fact, we are actually all one. This means that every single thing we do ultimately affects (and is felt by) every other person everywhere. In much the same way that a pebble thrown into a pond will create a number of tiny circles, which then ripple outward to touch and overlap one another, so too does every single 'small' act of self-empowerment impact every other person in the world. This is precisely what we do when we intentionally change any of our energy stamps.

The Energy Tube

Our Energy Tubes are at the very center of our energetic being. As mentioned earlier, this tube begins at the top of our heads and travels the entire length of our spinal column and all the way down to the ground beneath our feet. We 'feel' this tube quite often, for it is actually the seat of our emotions, which is why any alterations in this tube will always result in emotional turbulence. At the same time, however, using our emotions is the easiest way to intentionally effect changes in our tube.

The main purpose of the energy tube is to carry energy (and specifically the love energy) through our physical being and ground it into the Earth. As humans, our natural movement has been to take our creations from the ethereal realm, run them through this tube, and manifest them in physical reality. The problem is, most of the time, we do this by default on an unconscious level, which is why so many of us end up with things and situations that we do not want. Now, as we move forward in the new energy and learn to use higher forms of the love energy, we have the opportunity to evolve from being unconscious manifestors to becoming wholly conscious creators.

Fig 2

Creation process. Everything man-made first began as a thought form.

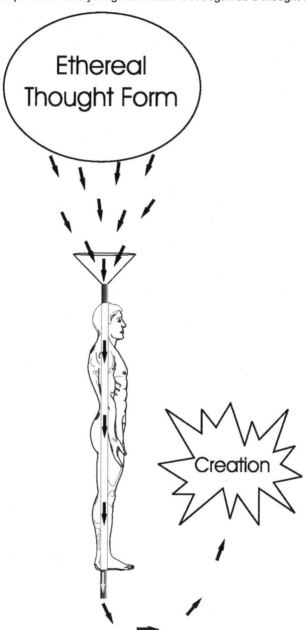

Expanding our Energy Tubes

Up to this point in time, owing to the thickness of the 'veil', our energy tubes have only been able to carry a certain range of energies. Thus our powers of creation have been somewhat limited. This is now changing, however, and our energy tubes are beginning to stretch in order to accommodate higher forms of energy. As we run these higher forms of energy, which I call 'light', through our energy tubes, it enlarges them and changes their attributes. This is what is responsible for the tremendous emotional stress so many people are feeling right now, because our emotions are our connection between our higher and lower selves.

The energy stamps that we receive as a result of our experiences are carried on the outside of our energy tubes. When an event happens that stamps its imprint on our energy tube, it is has a similar effect to what happens when we step on a garden hose, thereby impeding the free flow of water through the hose.

Whenever something makes you doubt yourself, or whenever you experience an incident or emotion that restricts your energy, the effect it has on your energy tube is just like crimping the garden hose. Every time you try to bring something from the ethers through that crimped tube, some of your energy will be restricted. This in turn hampers the manifestation of your creation. Not only that, but as your energy rubs the inside of the tube where it is crimped, it also stirs up a number of negative emotions and fears. It is this restriction, or crimping of your energy, that is actually responsible for the creation of the self-fulfilling prophecies, in which all your greatest fears become your reality.

All of the psychological modalities and therapies that are

so popular today are, of course, geared toward easing the pain of a crimped energy tube. The reason they are so popular is that many people are actually working very hard to open up, examine, and ultimately clear these areas so that they can consciously create through their tubes without being slaves to emotional pain.

While these therapies continue to work quite well, now that things are moving much faster, it's becoming even more important for us to clear our energy tubes, so that they are more capable of carrying more light. The challenge is that it is not possible for us to enlarge our energy tubes with any energy stamps still in place.

The key to true spiritual growth lies in doing whatever is necessary to facilitate the comfortable expansion of the energy tube.

Healing our energy stamps allows us to expand these energy tubes and thus, leads to growth as a spirit. Healing energy stamps is similar to healing any wound in that it rarely reverts back to its original state. Thus it is not uncommon for scar tissue to form where a crimp in a tube once was. This is not as bad as it sounds. For this scar tissue is the gift that we never wish to lose, as it is an indelible reminder of our brave journey through the experience of being human. It is a badge of mastery. The real problem lies in the fact that, for most of us, once an energy stamp has been healed, we prefer to put it behind us and forget it ever happened. While this is a personal choice, it does make it more difficult for us to take the next step in our evolution. Those who can wear their badges of mastered experience with pride usually find the next step much easier to negotiate.

Few would doubt that we have reached a time of rapid evolution for humankind. For most of us, our energy tubes are equally expanding in order to better accommodate this evolution. As they expand, the energy stamps imprinted on the outside of our tubes are likely to be activated. Even if they have been dealt with and only scar tissue remains, some of this scar tissue may also resurface as a direct result of our forward movement. This might cause some problems for many people, who, thinking they had dealt with most of their childhood issues, may find themselves becoming quite confused or self-critical. Many may not understand why, having made a conscious decision, followed by all the necessary efforts, to ascend to the next level, they should suddenly be troubled by having old mother, father, or abuse issues raising their ugly heads all over again.

Of course, those who have denied or effectively hid these core issues from themselves are naturally more likely to have them resurface with far greater intensity than if they had dealt with them in the first place.

If you (or your clients) feel this way, please know that this is simply a sign that your energy tube is expanding. Understand that, by its very nature, this type of expansion may result in experiencing some degree of emotional pain. Misery, on the other hand, is strictly an optional experience.

It may help to think of this like scar tissue on your skin. If you've ever taken a piece of scarred skin and tried to stretch it you will know that scar tissue is not as elastic as normal, healthy skin tissue, thus it is bound to cause some discomfort. The same is true of energy tubes. It may be helpful to keep in mind that expanding the energy tubes – and any parts that may be covered in scar tissue – will be far less painful compared with the original healing. You won't need years of therapy to deal with any negative emotions that may resurface, as these "shadow stamps" will re-heal very quickly.

Remember - the energy tube is the mid-point between your higher self and your lower self, or, to put it another way, your infinite, unlimited self, and your finite, restricted self. Since emotions span the gap between your higher and lower self, they cannot help but be felt most intensely along the energy tube itself. Because of this, the energy tube itself *is* the seat of your emotions, and this is precisely how this will be felt. . . through emotions.

This is also why this transition process may prove easier for women than it will for men, since most males have a greater tendency to hide or stifle their emotions, whereas most females are more adept and more comfortable with bringing them straight to the surface.

It is important to remember to not feel disillusioned if you find old issues resurfacing as you grow and evolve. Instead, try to view them as a sign that you are on your path, and concentrate on celebrating their release. For the more you release, the more room you will be creating for your energy tube to expand, and the more your energy tube expands, the more power you will have to manifest and ground all your future creations into reality.

Fig 3

Energy Stamps are carried on the energy tube, much like dents.

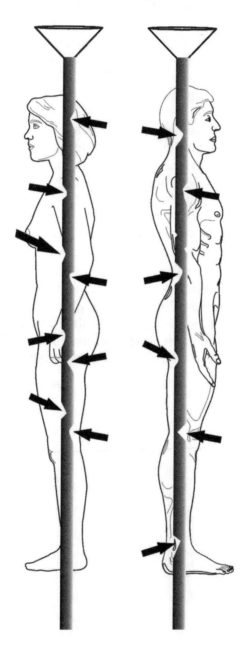

Fig 4
As the creative energy flows through the tube these dents, or restrictions, cause emotional pain.

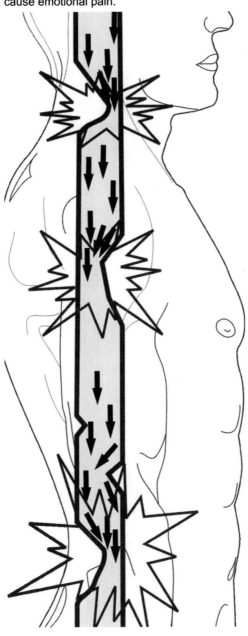

Fig 5

As our connection to our higher self steadily increases, both our
collector and tube expand to carry the increased energy. This can
create strain on any area of restriction, including scar tissue left
from previously healed energy stamps. This is why old issues often
resurface as we begin to evolve as spiritual beings.

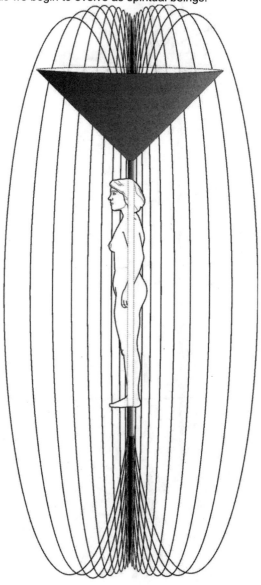

Chapter 7

Energy Matrix

•••

Energy Stamps

———

Two ways we facilitate our Primary Life Lessons

ENERGY

en·er·gy
Pronunciation: 'e-n&r-jE
Function: noun
1 a: dynamic quality (in motion) <narrative energy>
b: the capacity of acting or being active <intellectual energy>
2: vigorous exertion of power: EFFORT
<investing time and energy>
3: the capacity for doing work
4: usable power (as heat or electricity); also: the resources for producing such power

This chapter is not just about energy; rather, it explains the way our spirits deal with energy when we are in our bubbles of biology (Our physical bodies). Before coming to Earth, we set up our life lessons and determine what we will work on when we incarnate. Our intent is to achieve mastery. Sometimes we set up contracts that facilitate these lessons. Other times we set up situations that place us face-to-face with our life lessons. Once we begin to see ourselves from the perspective of pure energy, it becomes easier to see where we are and what we can do to move forward.

The following information was given to me during private sessions with individuals over five years. In these sessions I get to see people from an energy perspective. In other words, instead of getting wrapped up in clients' dramas, beliefs or the mechanics of their situation, I see things from a perspective of pure energy.

The Three Attributes of Energy

1. Energy is dynamic potential. It must move to exist. Merriam Webster defines dynamic as: "usually continuous and productive activity or change;" in other words, movement.

2. Energy *is*. It is not possible to create energy or to destroy it. It is only possible to convert it from one form to another. Energy can be stored temporarily as potential but it will always be seeking to complete a full circle of life.

3. The absence of everything reveals the base energy known as Universal Energy. This is the energy that binds all things together. The Universal Energy, from which all other energies are derived, is what we experience as unconditional love. In the spiritual realm this is the energy that we know to be the God energy.

We live in a constant sea of energy. Many of us feel this energy, and many have a profound sensitivity to various other forms of subtle energy. Some feel these energies so strongly that they are severely impacted by them. In the lower vibrations of the old energy it was possible to live in a location that did not support one's own energy. But in the higher vibrations, this could slowly drain a person's life force and lead to dis-ease. In the New Earth it is imperative that we all live in an energy that feeds our own.

Since our true essence is energy, our energy field makes up the essence of who we are. Because this is how we interface with the universe around us, it's very important to be aware of the things that can alter our energy field. Every experience and everything that enters our field alters us in some way. In fact, we are the sum total of all our experiences to date. This is what we refer to as our personality.

Our personality, or energy field, is carried with us from one lifetime to the next. To understand what this means, it's important to understand some of the basics about energy.

Magnetics

Magnetic energy is one of the least understood energies in our world, yet it affects us far more than many of us know. Magnetic energy flows in lines. When we place an object inside a magnetic field, some of the magnetic energy in that field will be transmuted into the object. The properties of the object itself will determine what form the energy takes.

It is the magnetic energy within the Earth that gives certain locations particular energy that feels so good to us. The magnetic lines that surround our planet – i.e., ley lines - can be sensed by many animals. This explains many species' uncanny sense of direction. This was proven in an experiment in which homing pigeons were fitted with small magnets on their heads, which interfered with the normal magnetic energy in the pigeons' location, thereby causing them to lose their sense of direction.

Animals know that by following the magnetic lines they can find their way home. As we are evolving, our own biology is adjusting to incorporate these same abilities. This is why many of us are suddenly feeling an inexplicable pull to relocate. Indeed, some of us are even finding ourselves drawn to parts of the country or areas of the world that may never previously have held any appeal for us.

Energy and our 'Bubbles of Biology'

We all know that one of the ways in which we derive energy is from the foods we eat. The food [energy] we consume converts from one form of energy to another.

Our own physical biology is merely a temporary conductor of energy. It is only by passing energy through this conductor that our biology maintains its form. If we were to cease passing energy through our biology, we would cease to exist.

There are many energy fields enveloping our 'bubbles of biology' that exert an effect on us. These energy fields actually create the form for our physical body in the etheric realms, thus we become whatever we create in these energy fields. A simple way of looking at this phenomenon is to say that we become what we *think*. Even conservative scientists are now beginning to accept that consciousness alters matter.

Our human experience, as it relates to energy, is now changing. Although we are moving into our Lightbody, it will still be necessary for energy to pass through our bodies. In order to understand what lies ahead of us, it may help to understand something of the true nature of our energetic structures.

Core Personality

Personality is that core essence that remains with a soul on both sides of the veil. We often confuse personality and energy stamps. Energy stamps are the result of events, lessons learned, and experiences gained in life. These can be positive or negative. Our core personality is the culmination of all experiences that we chose to incorporate in to our core personality. We cary this core soul personality with us into all future experiences and incarnations.

Our core personality stays with us even as we leave the life experience. It is the basis of who we really are. Those that speak to spirits on the other side of the veil know that even when they go home they still retain their core personality. Some even have the same sense of humor and the same personality as they had during their lifetime.

All levels of vibration are included in the core personality, including a signature smell or scent. This explains why so many people often smell a departed loved one's favorite fragrance. Many more are not consciously aware of the scent but it often awakens people from their dreams or triggers memories even as they are walking down the street. As we move forward in evolution, our sense of smell is becoming more acute. (In fact, many people are already telling me that they are becoming less tolerant to scents that they used to live with every day.) This will allow even more of this new form of communication and will help all of us listen more easily to spirit communication. This will also help us see the true core personality of a spirit.

Our core personality can most easily be understood as the special flavor of God that resides within each of us. However, the experiences and the energy stamps we receive during life have an effect on our core personality, sometimes altering it for the duration of a lifetime.

Upon leaving each life, our soul has the opportunity to choose which energy stamps it will integrate as part of its core personality. Any negative energy stamps received during a lifetime can be released upon returning Home. Since Home is an environment in which negative and positive energy do not exist, all energy stamps that we do not consciously choose to incorporate into our personality automatically dissolve when we make our transition.

Not only does our core personality contain all the life lessons we have mastered through the energy matrix, it also becomes more defined with each life lesson that we master. Once a vibrational level has been reached, you never return to a lower level. As energy stamps are released and energy matrices are mastered, the vibration of our soul increases to its original 'Om' vibration. When mastery of all life lessons is complete, our soul returns with its core personality fully expanded. This is the manner in which God can see God, thereby fulfilling the original purpose of the game.

One Rule

There is only one rule that we have placed upon this game board that we call life on Earth: free choice is always in effect, especially relating to the energy structures of human life. The energy matrix we choose before coming here determines the way we deal with energy. We choose contracts to provide ourselves with the experiences that stamp us with the energy necessary to facilitate mastery. However, it is important to note that this by no means determines our experience or the outcome of our own particular game. As these events and lessons unfold we have complete choice what to do with them. This is the nature of the game and the basis of our true power.

The Energy Matrix

The energy matrix controls much more of our game than we imagine. As we re-enter the game with each incarnation, we choose an energy matrix in which to house ourselves for the duration of our time in the Earth experience. This energy matrix is the energy vehicle in which we will experience our life. Our energy matrix determines how we deal with energy when it first enters our field. It's actually the way we are wired for energy. This is one of the main reasons that each of us reacts differently than one another in different circumstances.

There are twelve basic energy matrices. Each has different attributes and can facilitate different life lessons.

Much the way we may choose our sex from one lifetime to the next in order to facilitate life lessons, so also do we choose an energy matrix for each incarnation, continuing with that life lesson in successive incarnations until it is mastered.

Unlike an energy stamp, the attributes of an energy matrix never change within a lifetime. The life lesson will never facilitate changing or 'healing' an energy matrix. The fact that an energy matrix can never be healed is the primary reason that some people never respond to certain healing modalities, no matter how many sessions they have. The lesson with an energy matrix is to learn mastery of the matrix itself, thereby turning detriments into attributes.

How can you learn mastery of a matrix? Our definition of mastery is *finding positive uses for negative attributes.* When you master an energy matrix you learn to use its attributes to the highest outcome, as opposed to the lowest. Once mastered, you continue to use that mastered matrix for the remainder of that lifetime. The next lifetime you simply choose a different matrix that allows you to focus on other life lessons. Once mastered, a matrix never needs to be repeated as the mastery becomes part of your core personality and thus remains with you from one lifetime to the next.

When you master a life lesson through the use of an energy matrix, it does not mean that you will spend the rest of your life walking on water. It merely means that you have effectively found ways of utilizing what could otherwise be seen as negative attributes. Mastery is not a goal that is reached, but a way of life that is practiced over time. Since we live on a planet of free choice, however, even when we achieve mastery over several life lessons, we can always choose to fall back out of mastery. Although this is rare, when it does happen it is generally through neglect or inaction on our part.

Once mastery of a particular life lesson is experienced, the focus of our life is shifted toward repeating successful experiences in order to develop a life habit of mastery in the area of our present primary life lesson.

Even when we have achieved mastery of a specific life lesson, we still have the same energy matrix, and thus we will always have a bit of a blind spot in that particular area. For example, if we are working with a life lesson of Trust, we will always have a natural tendency to not trust ourselves, or to attract people into our field who have the potential to abandon us or otherwise pull the rug out from under our feet. Even though we have mastered the life lesson, we still may not be able to see this type of person coming. If we are working with an energy matrix with a life lesson of Definition, we will always have a tendency to attract master manipulators into our lives. Mastery does not change the attributes of an energy matrix; it only changes how we deal with it.

The other important thing about energy matrices is that once we have achieved mastery over them, we often move into teaching. This is not a prerequisite or requirement, and often is not even conscious. What happens is that we simply start sending out a different vibration, to which other people start responding. In most cases, the students just start showing up. The funny part is that very few of us actually teach about the primary life lesson we are mastering. Instead, most of us teach about some other area of passion in our lives, but somehow, within our teaching, the lessons are subtly conveyed.

Old Souls

Once several matrices have been mastered, the veil begins to grow very thin. 'Old Souls' are people who have become very good at mastering energy matrices.

Many times we will look into the eyes of infants and see the wisdom and the mastery they have brought back with them. As parents, it is our job to help these old souls remember their mastery. These seasoned veterans have incorporated many energy stamps into their core personality over many lifetimes. They have well defined personalities and this is why we recognize them so easily. It is these innate qualities of Definition that often catapult them into the public eye. We love to watch them because we can see part of ourselves in them.

Last Timers

Once we have mastered between eight and ten energy matrices we can choose to be finished with the game on Earth and move into other spheres of existence. Even though there may still be life lessons to master, our increasing skill at the mastery process makes life on Earth so much easier that it often begins to lose its attraction.

Now that children are being born with higher attributes, such as the Indigo and Crystal Children, many of us who could move on are rediscovering our appetite for, and attraction to, the game and choosing to return. In fact, many last timers have chosen to return to Earth at this time specifically to participate in the exciting evolutionary process that is now unfolding.

Energy Stamps

Energy stamps are a particular form of energy that gets imprinted on us through certain experiences during a particular lifetime. Energy stamps can be positive or negative. Like an energy matrix, we agree to carry energy stamps to facilitate life lessons for ourselves. The stamps are carried on the energy tube that runs throughout our body. (See the chapter on 'Clearing the

Energy Tubes') Unlike the energy matrix, however, we can heal and release energy stamps. It is not necessary to carry negative energy stamps throughout our entire lifetime, although many do choose to do precisely that. Positive energy stamps, on the other hand, become quickly incorporated into the core personality. Once a life lesson associated with a particular energy stamp is complete, it is a simple matter to rewrite the script and so create a new perspective on events.

Catalysts

Whether you choose to facilitate a primary life lesson through an energy matrix or through receiving an energy stamp, a catalyst is generally required to activate the lesson. Catalysts are more predominant when working with energy stamps than when working with an energy matrix, as it is usually the catalyst that imprints one with the first energy stamp. Still, a catalyst is generally present in both.

For example, in the case of a life lesson of Adaptation, you may place yourself in a family where your father has a job that requires constant relocation throughout your childhood. In this case, the catalyst for your life lesson would be your father who is responsible for stamping, or imprinting, you with the repeated experience of not having a solid foundation at home. In a life lesson of Trust, you may choose to be born to an abusive or absent mother so that you can learn to trust your own energy to support your spirit. In a life lesson of Communication, you might choose a father who can easily speak and express his thoughts, but does not seem to be able to ever tell *you* that he loves you. In each case these family members would serve as the important catalysts who activate your life lesson for you. In each case, the roles of catalyst would have been agreed in advance, as you made contracts with the various people involved during the planning stages of your life.

Although energy stamps do not have to be carried forward from one lifetime to the next, it is possible (but not very common) to set up a genetic predisposition for carrying a particular energy stamp through several lifetimes in order to facilitate a specific lesson. For example, if a soul does not heal a negative energy stamp in one lifetime they may choose to carry it forward as an energy predisposition to be healed in a future lifetime. Many times a soul will place themselves in an energy line that is very similar to a genetic line. Although there is no predetermination in these energy lines, there is a predisposition that can help to reinstall an energy stamp in the next lifetime.

The Sins of the Fathers

When we heal and release an energy stamp, we heal it backward and forward in the linear timeline.

Here's an example: Envision a family of four - husband, wife, and a male and a female child. When the husband was young, his father used to beat him because he wanted his son to be the best he could be. Now, as a result of the energy stamp which his father gave him in those beatings, this man carries a hidden anger deep within. This anger eats away at him, and with no appropriate way to vent this negative energy, he finds it erupting at the most inappropriate times. Now, let us say that he occasionally turns to alcohol to relax. He soon finds that this gives him a way to vent and take his power, or so he thinks. Pretty soon, he starts drinking more and more in order to feel better about his actions. Before long, he's become totally reliant on alcohol as a form of release. One day this man comes home to find his wife angry that he is once again intoxicated. In the ensuing argument the anger he's been suppressing all his life finally erupts and he physically abuses his wife. Now the energy is in motion.

Even if the children are not at home when this event takes place, and even if it is never mentioned, they become stamped with this same energy. As time goes on the male child will most likely grow up and experience anger problems himself. As much as he determines to not be like his father, it may not be long before he finds himself in a similar situation. Because of the energy stamps, he is also likely to make similar choices. Thus, not only may he end up repeating his father's pattern of 'self-medicating' his wound with alcohol, it's very likely he also may abuse his wife too.

Likewise, the daughter in this family may grow up with an unconscious need to attract people into her life who will place her in the role of victim. She may not be able to figure out why she is attracted to abusive relationships, but still the pattern repeats itself over and over again. And so it continues, with 'the sins of the father' being visited on each successive generation until some member of this family makes a conscious choice to break the chain and do the inner work necessary to release this energy stamp. When this happens, the energy stamp is instantly healed, both backward and forward in time. This means that not only is this situation healed for the son or daughter, it also gets healed for the parents and grandparents as well.

In other words, instead of replicating his father's actions, this young man could not only change his own behavior, but his father's behavior would also magically alter as he, too, begins to soften. At the same time, the young man's own children will no longer need to experience the effects of an energy stamp that may have been unconsciously passed down for many generations.

Planning the Life Lesson

When we are planning each incarnation in our first stage of life there are a number of ways we can set up the experiences we need in order to reach mastery of that life lesson. For example, we could choose our experiences through contracts with love relationships, catalysts, children, business relationships and many other potential connections. Even though we set up these contracts to intentionally put us in the perfect position to experience opportunities for mastery, all contracts come to us in one of two ways; either they come through the experience of an energy stamp or they come through the wiring of an energy matrix.

Furthermore, while it is possible to be working with both an energy matrix and an energy stamp in some situations, just like being right or left handed, we will generally tend to lean one way or the other to facilitate our primary life lesson. Although our contracts will play out the same, the actual manner in which we master our life lesson will depend on whether we have chosen an energy matrix or an energy stamp to facilitate it.

Certain primary attributes of life allow Spirit to see itself in physical form. Once mastered, these attributes lead to a mastery of self and an incorporation of the higher self within the core personality. Up to this point in evolution, our advancement has been quite slow when measured by our own standards. It used to be very common for souls to choose life lessons and set up certain experiences, only to find they looked the other way when the appointed time came. In fact, it was quite usual for a person to incarnate as many as one hundred lifetimes to work on a single phase of a primary life attribute and still not get it.

Until recently there were relatively few masters. In the last fifty years, however, the game has changed rapidly, and we have now begun to awaken and take our own power. Because of the higher vibration we're now living in, it has become possible for us to resolve and master our life lessons more rapidly, thus allowing more of us to achieve mastery of the all twelve primary life lessons. Indeed, many of us have advanced more in the last year than we may have done over several previous lifetimes. We should be proud of ourselves for this advancement, for it reflects our own power of choice. It is our collective attainment of these higher vibrations that has led to the present release of the information in this book.

Karma

The score-keeping system of karma has enabled us to see exactly where we are in the process up to now. We designed this elaborate system for the express purpose of measuring our own individual advancement. Because of our connection to each other, it also facilitated family karma, group karma and long-term karma, all of which have enabled humanity to reach the new levels we are attaining. Now, however, that old score keeping system is no longer valid or necessary.

Humans are advancing at an astounding rate and new measuring systems are needed. A new direct cause and effect system is now in place that can (but hopefully will no longer) be carried forward from one lifetime to the next. The main difference is that now the reaction is very rapid. Karma within groups, and long-term karma (karma which has often been handed down through generations) has been released, since, in this higher state, it is no longer needed to accomplish the advancement of humanity. Even with karmic release, however, many are so accustomed to it that they still act as if it is in place, thereby unwittingly creating a vicious and unnecessary cycle of cause and effect.

The Way it Works

In the planning session preceding each incarnation, we each decide which life lessons we will work on. We assign roles and make specific contracts for our life experience. Many times these are repeat performances. For instance, there may be a spouse from your last incarnation that will be here at the same time and you decide to connect again. Perhaps we experienced a great love last time round, but failed to attain the level of communication that we wished to achieve, thus, we may agree to return and resume our relationship in order to complete the connection.

In most cases, these planning sessions are fairly elaborate as we plan many alternate possibilities at the same time. Since this is the planet of free choice, we obviously need to create many back-up plans in case we should elect not to activate a particular contract or previously planned course of action, one that may be crucial to our life lesson. Many contracts do not get chosen. This isn't right or wrong, it's just a choice, and all choices are honored.

Generally there are many different phases of life lessons that we may choose to complete. For example, in order to learn the art of Creation, we may choose to approach the lesson through several different contracts and experiences. We may even plan several experiences to occur simultaneously, just to make sure.

When working on an especially important lesson, we will often choose during our planning session to place a particular experience in our path in such a manner that it is impossible to ignore. Even with these elaborate set-ups, it is still possible for us to become so caught up in our 'victimhood' that we completely disregard our responsibility for the lesson, and walk right by. When we experience this kind of lesson, the energy is stamped upon our energy tube so forcefully that it will remain with us until we choose either to heal it or to integrate it. In the event of the latter, it is possible for us to choose in the final stage of life (acclimation) to carry this energy stamp forward to our next lifetime. We do this by carrying the energy stamp in our cellular memory, and also by creating an experience in our next lifetime that will ensure that particular energy stamp is imprinted upon us again. Thus, even though many energy stamps have their origins in previous lifetimes, this ensures we have everything in the current lifetime that we need for healing it.

When we are in the first stage of life planning our experience, we are able to see the larger picture. In fact, in the past it was common for us to set up a whole series of events designed to occur over many lifetimes. Although we generally choose a single life lesson to focus on in any given lifetime, we also are constantly reinforcing life lessons mastered in previous lifetimes.

In situations where we attempted to work on a life lesson through a series of energy stamps and still failed to master it over a number of lifetimes, we will often switch to an energy matrix to help facilitate mastery of the lesson. As some life lessons lead naturally into others, it is also common for us to set up a long-term path that's designed to help us master several successive life lessons.

Since the energy matrix was formed to facilitate the advanced game we're currently playing on the new planet earth, it has only been in use for a relatively short period of time. Prior to this, energy stamps were our only means of moving forward.

Energy matrices are subtle energy fields that are not yet measurable with current technology. At this stage of our technology, it is popularly believed that a strong energy field has more effect than a weak or subtle energy field.

Owing to this basic human belief, very little research has been conducted with subtle energy fields. When these studies do begin, it is my belief that we will understand much more about the construction of the energy matrix.

Chapter 8

The 12 Primary Life Lessons

———————

Paths to Mastery

We work to master twelve primary life attributes in our experience as humans. With each lifetime, we choose one primary life lesson to work with, and continue to work on it in consecutive lives until we achieve mastery of that single attribute. Then we move on to choose another primary life lesson to work with in the following incarnation. In the past, we generally only worked with one primary life lesson at a time. There are certain instances where we may work with two or more, but most of the time we have confined ourselves to only one. For instance, if people come very close to mastering a life lesson at the end of a lifetime but don't quite achieve full mastery, they may choose to continue working on it as a secondary life lesson in their next incarnation.

When a facilitator is assisting clients to identify their primary life lesson, it is important to know that there are no hard and fast rules. For example, a woman who grew up with sexual abuse as a child will not always be working with a life lesson of Trust, even though this form of abuse provides a perfect foundation for learning Trust. She may, in fact, be working with a life lesson of Acceptance, or Definition, or even Love.

Similarly, an individual's persona and behavior will change dramatically with each step they take towards achieving mastery of their life lesson. For example, a person working with a life lesson of Charity is generally very sensitive but in order to protect themselves they often unconsciously disconnect from others. This will make them appear as if they are extremely selfish and interested only in themselves. Yet, once they begin to reach a higher level of mastery they will become more comfortable with displaying their sensitivity towards others. People will think they have changed but all that has really happened is that they have evolved as a result of the work they have done. An interesting side note here is that in such cases the person themselves will not recognize that they have changed.

Because there are no hard and fast rules I have included a number of case studies from my own files as templates to help illustrate how differently the patterns associated with each life lesson may be played out. I have found these templates very useful when helping clients understand why they are a certain way, or why they keep repeating the same 'mistakes' over and over again. This gives the clients a good overview of their entire life experience which helps them make more effective choices. Once a person learns that they have a blind spot (which they themselves set up to help facilitate this life lesson), they can take steps to compensate for this when similar circumstances present themselves in the future.

Human Evolution

There is no doubt that humanity is evolving at an astounding rate. The Group suggests that most of us have advanced as souls more in the last six years than we have in the last six lifetimes. To differentiate between these different levels of evolution I use the terms higher and lower vibration. It's important to note that this is not actually a vibration that can be physically measured in the body, but rather, could be best described as a state of mind. When people become interested in seeking a deeper meaning to life, they are actually raising their overall state of awareness. This is what I mean when I refer to raising their vibrational level. Here again, however, it is important to bear in mind that one vibrational level is not better than another, they are merely different. In the same way that the sixth grade is not better than the third grade, so too is a 'higher vibration' not better than a 'lower vibration'.

So, if we are advancing so rapidly what effect does this have on the Twelve Primary Life Lessons? Actually the

Twelve Primary Life Lessons have been around as long as we have. But whereas we used to take anything between sixty and one hundred lifetimes to master a single life lesson, our rapid evolution has now made it possible for us to accomplish this in a single lifetime. But we can only do so if we are aware of the higher purpose of this game that we have chosen to play.

Warning

With this in mind, let us never forget that even those life lessons that may look particularly disgusting, might have a purpose that ultimately benefits us all. The person panhandling on a street corner, the homeless person rifling through a trash can for food, even the thief or murderer that repels us may, in fact, already have achieved mastery of many more life lessons than we will ever know.

This helps us to remember that with our limited vision none of us have the overall perspective to judge another soul on their path. The person we may be looking at with such abhorrence may be a master who has returned to start working on their final life lesson. The reality is, if you see something or someone that is particularly repellent to you, this generally means that they are working on a primary life lesson that you have laready mastered. Thus, there is a natural intolerance and even a sensivity to these attributes.

Young Adults and Children

I have used this information about the Twelve Primary Life Lessons with children on several occasions with interesting results. Many parents book sessions with me solely to gain greater insights into their children. Some can't understand why their children don't respond in typical ways. In many instances, I've then been asked to have a session with their child in the hope that this information will benefit them too. Interestingly, I have found that my sessions with teenagers and younger children are generally substantially shorter than the session I have with most adults.

I have found that a 45-minute session is usually ample for me to explain the overview of a person's life and plant the necessary seeds. With young people, however, this can usually be accomplished in around twenty minutes or so. Part of the reason is that young people's life experiences are obviously much shorter and, therefore, they've had less time to develop the behavioral patterns associated with their life lessons. Also, children born in the last thirty years are more advanced and, therefore, process in entirely different ways and at an entirely different rate than previous generations. These children, who have been labeled Indigo and Crystal children, are much quicker and more direct than most adults are. In order to catch their attention, information must be honed down to its very essence.

In recent years we have been seeing a vast increase in the number of children with learning challenges, such as ADD and ADHD. In my experience, many of these conditions are simply the result of children being born with advanced attributes in a society that is not ready for them. Even though many of these children may appear to have difficulty at school, they are actually very bright. In fact, the biggest challenge for these advanced humans is boredom.

When it comes to the Twelve Primary Life Lessons, I have found that most young people intuitively understand what I am saying. Even though they may not yet have had the chance to see the underlying patterns of their actions, they are generally aware of their weak points or blind spots. They simply need someone who can help them understand why they don't fit in. I have found that I don't need to spend much time explaining their patterns and contracts.

Instead, I tend to talk more about their blind spots and introduce ideas for how to deal with issues that will most likely crop up in the near future.

About Responsibility

One human attribute that is not listed here is responsibility. That's because responsibility is actually the *result* of an action, rather than an attribute in itself. It is the resulting action of mastering, or not mastering, as the case may be, life lessons. In other words, one either takes responsibility for working on one's life lesson, or one doesn't. The action of responsibility generally shows up in the life lessons of Be-ing, Creation, Trust, and, most common of all, Truth.

Collective Life Lessons

Life lessons are always personal in that they are always focused on the individual. However, many life lessons have also been facilitated by groups of people who have contracted to master the lesson collectively. For instance, certain socioeconomic or religious groups have created specific conditions purely in order to facilitate a particular life lesson. Let's say that you wanted to work with a life lesson of Acceptance. This could be facilitated much more easily if you were to place yourself in a black community in Alabama in the 1960's when racial discrimination was at its height in the United States. Likewise, being born into any poor family would provide the perfect conditions for mastering the life lessons of Trust, Creation or Adaptation.

In all instances we not only choose the best circumstances to facilitate each life lesson, we also place ourselves in precisely the most appropriate era. Let me explain. When we are in the first stage of life, planning our life contracts and set-ups, we have the ability to see the direction in which things are heading, and thus can place ourselves in exactly the right point in the timeline that will provide us with the best conditions to work on a specific life lesson. As an example, in the early 1920's, the most common life lesson was that of Charity, which concerns learning about our connection to other people. We chose to work on this lesson at that time because we saw that the Great Depression that lay ahead offered us the best opportunity to strengthen our connections to each other by helping one another through those difficult times. In the 1960's we collectively worked on the life lessons of Communication and Love. Today, there are many diverse groups working as collectives on different life lessons. Because the way we typically advance is to act like a pendulum, swinging from one extreme to another, we have swung from working collectively on the life lesson of Charity, to working collectively on the life lesson of Definition. The reason for this is because working on Charity not only taught us to recognize and honor our connection to each other, but also to think of others before we thought of ourselves. Now the pendulum is swinging in the other direction, we are finding that we have become so wrapped up in taking care of others that we have forgotten to think of ourselves. Thus, the collective life lesson of Definition is necessary right now to help us learn to place ourselves first.

It is also common for a family blood line to have a general attraction to specific life lessons. You will find that some families seem to pass down life lessons through generations almost as if it were genetic. This is known as lineage intent. Many times in the first stage of life we place ourselves in a specific blood line because the lineage intent will help us facilitate a lesson we are working on.

Definition is often a product of lineage intent and is most common among healers. In many ways it is like being born into a family of healers. It is the tremendous sensitivity that is an attribute of this life lesson which makes it possible for healers to facilitate healing for others.

It is only when people begin to master this life lesson by learning to place themselves first, and defining where their energy ends and another's begins, that they can fully step into their healing work.

In the old paradigm when we were taking between sixty and one hundred lifetimes to master one life lesson, we had no use for knowledge of the Twelve Primary Life Lessons. Now that we have started to advance very rapidly, however, this knowledge is becoming extremely helpful to the evolution of our species.

Relationships and the
Twelve Primary Life Lessons

Relationships can be the most challenging of all human experiences. To hold someone so close that you can see every detail of your own reflection is both extremely rewarding as well as extremely difficult.

In this section I will not attempt to deal with relationships in general, as that is the topic of a future book. Instead, we will look at the ways in which the Twelve Primary Life Lessons affect the establishment and growth of our relationships.

As previously stated, the general appearance of a person has a lot to do with where they are at in the mastery process of their primary life lesson. For instance, people working with a life lesson of Trust will appear shy and reserved in the early stages. Once they start to attain mastery, however, these people's demeanor will appear to be quite confident. The same rule applies to relationships. If two people are both working on their individual life lessons simultaneously, they will have a tendency to grow together. But if they are working on their primary life lessons at different rates they will more than likely grow apart. That said, the gaps that often occur during these difficult times could be bridged if the couple can communicate openly with one another.

Certain life lessons usually tend to attract counterparts inside relationships. For instance, I have seen the life lessons of Definition and Communication being worked on by many couples.

The real challenge in relationships occurs when one partner starts advancing rapidly in their life lesson and the other person makes no forward movement at all, or, worse, resents their partner's growth. Even though all other areas of such a relationship may be healthy, the differences in advancement will place these two people at vastly different vibrational levels. This will almost certainly cause great strain on the relationship, and quite often will lead to the breakdown of the relationship altogether. Even where both partner's commitment is strong enough to hold the relationship together, outside forces will often conspire to push them apart if they continue to remain at different vibrational levels for a prolonged period. This is the origin of the 'Bump' contract described in the chapter on The Nature of Contracts.

The reality is that not all relationships are meant to be for the long term. This is just as true of some successful relationships as it is of many difficult ones. I have seen many relationships that have just run their course and were complete, but neither party was willing to walk away from what was familiar to them and face the unknown. Take the case of Vera, for example.

When Vera had her first sessions with me, she told me she had been married for 41 years. "Congratulations," I said.

"No. Don't congratulate me," she said, "41 years is about twenty years too long."

According to Vera, the sex had stopped about twenty years before. The emotional intimacy had ceased even earlier than that, right around the time Vera had given birth to her youngest daughter, who was now thirty years old. Vera's children had been encouraging her to leave the relationship for some time before she decided to consult me.

Vera was working with a primary life lesson of Trust and a secondary life lesson of Definition. This meant that the hardest thing for her to do was to put herself first, and the most difficult word for her to say was 'no.' Vera knew where she was going, and what she would do when she got there. Nonetheless, she found that taking the first step and confronting her husband was unthinkable.

Eight months and another two sessions later, Vera finally left her husband and her house. At first she was terrified. But the support she received from those around her almost overwhelmed her with joy. Three weeks later her husband even called her to congratulate her on speaking her truth. One month after that, another interesting and significant event occurred.

One day, when Vera's husband was at his office, she returned to the marital home to collect some of her clothes. Without warning, she came face to face with her husband. After several minutes of chit-chat, Vera built up her courage, took a deep breath, and, in as nice a manner as she could, told him how strong and empowered she was feeling now that she was finally learning how to stand on her own two feet and put her own needs first. For the first time in her life, Vera stood completely in her truth and spoke from her heart. She no longer cared what others might think. This was her life, and she was going to live it for herself in the best and most productive way she knew how. Interestingly, by taking her own power and standing firm in her new sense of self, Vera had suddenly become extremely attractive to her ex-husband and they made love that day. It was unlike any lovemaking they had ever known before; for the first time in a long while their souls connected in a totally unhampered manner.

Vera never did return to her husband. As far as she was concerned, their contract was complete, and it was now time to move on. Even today, when people ask Vera about her ex-husband, she smiles mysteriously.

The Twelve Primary Life Lessons

1. Acceptance
2. Adaptation
3. Be-ing (Wholeness)
4. Charity
5. Communication (From the Heart)
6. Creation (Holding Power)
7. Definition (Centering your own Energy)
8. Integrity
9. Love
10. Trust
11. Truth (Self)
12. Grace

As you read through the above list you may have felt a tug at one or more of the attributes listed. These tugs generally indicate areas that you are working on in this lifetime. Until recently we only worked on one primary life lesson at a time, sometimes working on that lesson up to one hundred lifetimes without mastering it. Because of our recent advancement, however, it is now possible to master a primary life lesson the first time round. In fact, it is now becoming quite common for us to combine life lessons and work on two or more primary life lessons in a single lifetime. This is somewhat akin to a student at college choosing one subject to 'major' in as the focus of their degree and possible future career, and also selecting another subject as a secondary focus of their studies. With life lessons, many of us are choosing to concentrate most of our energies on mastering one primary life lesson, while at the same time focusing a lesser amount of energy on working on a secondary life lesson. In most cases, however, the secondary, or 'minor,' life lesson will rarely be completed in its entirety during one lifetime.

As you read on, you may become aware of a deep sense of familiarity with or recognition of some of the attributes described below. These are life lessons that you have mastered in this or previous lifetimes. Rarely do we feel as though we have mastered all twelve life lessons. Moreover, because we have total free choice in all matters, it is possible that we may sometimes even regress on some items that we have previously mastered, in which case we would need to re-master that particular attribute. However, since this would be done as a secondary life lesson, it would be facilitated a lot more speedily than it was the first time around.

At this point I should also caution you that you will almost certainly see yourself in several, and possibly even all, of the primary life lessons. It's important to keep in mind here that when we are working on these life lessons, they are naturally so personal to us that it's virtually impossible for us to be objective about our own experience. We have a built in blind spot when it comes to our own life lesson. For this reason, it is often helpful to have an objective outsider or facilitator to assist you in identifying your own primary life lesson. Once identified, it becomes much easier to see how all the major events in your life lead back to this one, or sometimes two, blind spots.

What follows is a description of the Twelve Primary Life Lessons, each of which is accompanied by one or two examples, based on real life cases from my client files, to help provide you with an illustration of the different ways these life lessons can play out.

In the interests of client confidentiality, I have used pseudonyms to protect the identities of the people concerned.

If any of these twelve attributes seems to be a recurring challenge in your own life, be aware that there is a good possibility that it is a life lesson that you are currently mastering.

The key to mastering each of the twelve Life attributes lies in discovering its higher purpose. As you read through each of the life lessons, first determine whether this feels like an energy matrix or an energy stamp. If it is an energy stamp, the key to healing and releasing it will be found within the life experience that created the stamp. If it is an energy matrix, remember, this is an attribute that can never be healed; it can only be mastered.

Throughout the following descriptions, I shall contrast the sexes in order to illustrate polarity.

We have all played roles as both male and female. The gender we choose for each incarnation is dictated by a number of factors, not the least of which are the life attributes we wish to master. There are many women who carry more male energy than most men, and vice versa. In the future, we will see more of a blending of these energies; the more we move toward unity consciousness, the more the energy gap between the sexes will begin to close.

Primary Life Lesson #1

Acceptance

Self Esteem or Self Acceptance and the Art of Graceful Acceptance

Although it is not restricted to it, this life lesson is most often experienced in female form.

If there is a negative catalyst in this life lesson people can become habituated to seeing themselves as a victim and then get caught up in that drama.

Energy blocks in this area may manifest as self-sabotage, whereby a person will appear to 'do everything right, but still nothing seems to work.' The person can learn to create quite well but as the energy they transmit starts returning to them, they have difficulty accepting the rewards.

Outwardly, these people may appear to be suffering from a general lack of self-esteem, but the underlying reason for this is due to a belief system that they are unworthy. If this belief system stems from an energy stamp it can be rewritten and changed by uncovering the origin and then working consciously to change the script. If it is part of their energy matrix, it can only be mastered through learning the Art of Graceful Acceptance and understanding that energy is a flow and not a destination.

Acceptance is the art of allowing energy to flow through you. By definition, energy does not exist if it does not move. Until energy starts moving it is purely a potential. In the experiences of life the ability of your spirit to feel comfortable in your 'bubble of biology' will be directly related to the amount of energy that flows through you. This is the Art of Graceful Acceptance.

If you look carefully at the areas where energy is blocked in your life, you may recognize that Acceptance may be the missing piece. The dear souls who choose Acceptance as a primary life lesson may have difficulty taking responsibility for their own reality. They see things as they believe them to be in two dimensions. Since this energy matrix often is best facilitated with feminine energy, it is not uncommon for these gentle people to set up contracts to become victims. They often have difficulty making sense of events and experiences, and may subconsciously harbor very deep resentments towards others. Acceptance can be a difficult attribute to master, for once a life pattern is set it is difficult to change it. Even when people claim full responsibility for creating their own reality, they can still be stuck in specific patterns that conspire to provide a steady supply of people willing to victimize them in one way or another.

This is not just about those who are victims, however. The lesson of Acceptance can manifest in many different ways and areas. For example, a recurring pattern of money problems can indicate that people have still not learned how to accept. They may be adept at sending out all the energy required to start the flow moving in their direction, yet when that energy returns full circle, they find it difficult to accept the abundance it brings.

If you are facilitating others or are working with Acceptance as a primary energy matrix yourself, it's important to start allowing energy to flow through you in every possible way. Look for areas where the energy may be stuck and work to release it. Practice the Art of Graceful Acceptance. Get good at accepting. (See more about this in the chapter The Five Traditions of Abundance in Welcome Home ~ The New Planet Earth. by Lightworker books]

Another important aspect of this life lesson is the acceptance of responsibility. Responsibility is the balance to personal power. The equation is simple: If you wish to create more success in your personal life, then you must accept more personal responsibility for your own happiness. Likewise, if you wish to create more success in your relationships, you must take more responsibility for building the relationship. For example, those always looking for their soul mate and their perfect match will have less success in relationships than those who consciously work to nurture and transform what may seem like a less than perfect match into a relationship that works for them.

Case History No. 1

Name: Shirley
Age: 41
Marital Status: Divorced
Profession: Massage Therapist/Healer
Life Lesson: Acceptance
Catalyst: Mother
Type: Energy Matrix

Shirley first contacted me for a reading when she was 41. A divorcee with a grown son whom she appeared to be completely dissociated from, Shirley was not a very happy woman. She couldn't understand why, whenever she got settled in a place, something disastrous always seemed to happen to necessitate moving on. She had moved her home fifteen times in the three years following her divorce, each time to a different city or town. One landlord decided to sell the house she was renting, another home she lived in burned down, a third place that had seemed perfectly fine when she moved in suddenly required extensive work to be done on the building. Time after time the rug kept being pulled out from under her. At one point, she even ended up living out of her car. It wasn't that she didn't have friends who would put her up; there were lots of places Shirley could have stayed while she got back on her feet again, but she was a proud woman who didn't like asking favors or being beholden to or dependent upon others. Other areas of her life were relatively normal, yet Shirley did not have a place she could call home.

At first glance, one might think that Shirley was unconsciously sabotaging herself, but this wasn't the case – at least not directly. What I was shown during our telephone session was that Shirley was working on a life lesson of Acceptance. In order to facilitate this life lesson Shirley had to set up some specific contracts and experiences ahead of time that would ensure she attracted the necessary opportunities to see the purpose for what was happening around her and change it.

In Shirley's case, it worked like this: Shirley's mother, who had agreed to play the role of catalyst in this situation, firmly believed that the greatest success one could achieve in life was to own a home. This is what had been drummed into Shirley since childhood. Although this seems to be an energy stamp, Shirley was actually working with an energy matrix and was simply wired for this life lesson. Her mom had simply imprinted Shirley from infancy as part of her agreement to act as the catalyst for Shirley's chosen life lesson. This became obvious when Shirley attempted to change the role of her mother in her life. She did so yet still had the same challenges as before. When working with an energy matrix it is only possible to master the attributes that you already have.

Having absorbed this imprinted belief system, Shirley's challenge was to learn to *accept* the exact opposite – i.e., that 'success,' for her, had nothing to do with her mother's criterion. Hence, she was always unconsciously looking for ways to work with self-acceptance. Learning to accept that she was not bound by other people's definitions was a critical factor for Shirley in developing the necessary self-esteem to know that she *can* create the life she wants for herself. Becoming comfortable with change is an important step in this direction, because in doing so, Shirley would finally learn to become comfortable with her self, which, of course, is the very essence of self-acceptance. Once Shirley achieves this she will finally settle in one place.

The last time I heard from Shirley, she still had not mastered this life lesson. She was still bouncing between different houses and apartments in different cities and towns, with each subsequent circumstance becoming progressively more painful, and more 'in her face,' than the one before.

Note the patterns here, and what they all stem from and lead back to. Shirley's primary life lesson is Acceptance. Specifically, *self*-acceptance. In order to facilitate this, she had to have a catalyst (her mother) to activate her with a belief system that cannot help but conspire to reinforce her lack of self-esteem. Because she cannot accept herself, Shirley is incapable of accepting that others could find her loveable. Hence, she continually (albeit unconsciously) rejects both her husband and her son, which in turn, ultimately leads to divorce from the former and estrangement from the latter. These two events then become the trigger for the next phase, which is the manifestation of the strange series of disasters that guarantee Shirley never gets to puts down any roots, or establish any form of stability in her life.

If Shirley does ever get out of the loop she is stuck in, and starts to develop self-acceptance, not only will she learn to accept the flow of change in her life, but also her sense of self will become so strong that she will understand that it's not important *where* she lives because her security lies *within* her. Then she will have successfully mastered this difficult life lesson. The irony is, once she reaches this stage, Shirley will very likely wind up manifesting the very thing that her mother saw as being most important – her own home. There's a second irony here. And this is, that when Shirley gets her own home, it won't be nearly as important to her as it would have been to her mother.

Case History No. 2

Name: Jane
Age: 32
Marital Status: Widowed
Profession: Recording Artist
Life Lesson: Acceptance
Catalyst: Father
Type: Energy Stamp

Jane is a vibrantly beautiful young woman who seemed to have it all: a happy marriage to a man who not only adored her but also earned enough money to ensure that she and their young son had everything they could ever want. Then, out of the blue, tragedy struck. Jane's husband and young son died in a car crash. Jane wasn't in the car with them at the time.

Now that has to be one of the worst things that life can throw at you. How do you accept this? How do you move beyond the terrible grief of losing the two people you love the most in the world, and the future you'd planned together? How does one even begin to find the gift in it? At this point Jane had a few options: She could have taken refuge in victimhood, which would have been easy to do, or she could have sunk into a deep depression, which would have been totally understandable. Or she could have chosen to become very angry. In fact, Jane could have gotten stuck (as so many do) in any one or several of the ten stages of grief.

Mastery is the art of taking a negative situation, one that is way below the line of what we would consider normal, and finding a way to turn it around so that it leads to something positive. Today, this young lady is a professional singer and has released two popular CD's. What Jane did was to use the deep emotion of her loss to express her grief, and in so doing created something beautiful. This wasn't easy for Jane. Along with her husband, son, and her future, she had lost her financial security. For the first time in her life, she was thrown back entirely on her own resources. She had to learn how to take care of and support herself. While she'd always enjoyed singing as a hobby, it had never occurred to her that she could make a career out of it. Because she had to support herself somehow, Jane found a job, and began writing songs and singing in her spare time as a way of vocalizing her pain and working through the grieving process. After some time had passed, Jane then took the very risky and very courageous step of quitting her job in order to concentrate on recording her first CD.

While it's hard to believe that one would set up such tragic situations for oneself in order to facilitate a life lesson, that's precisely what Jane had done. The original catalyst for this life lesson had been her father, who had, albeit unwittingly, been the cause of Jane's lack of belief in herself. Because he had loved her so much, Jane's dad had wanted to spare her the pain of disappointment. And while he had always loved and praised her singing voice, he'd voiced it in such a way that it made her feel as though she wasn't really good enough. "That's nice, honey," he'd say, "go ahead and sing if you want to, but don't set your sights too high, because there are lots of people out there who are much better than you." In attempting to protect her, Jane's father had actually imprinted her with an energy stamp that ensured Jane grew up with very little belief in her abilities and, thus, a chronic lack of self-acceptance and self-esteem.

The tragic deaths of Jane's husband and son then acted as the triggers that would set into motion the challenges Jane needed to overcome in order to master this life lesson.

Primary Life Lesson #2

Adaptation

Change

Our natural physiology is capable of great change in a very short time period. It is our physical form that often resists change. Therefore, we don't cope well with change.

The life lesson of Adaptation is about learning to adjust and to become comfortable with change. Few of us are comfortable with change, because it represents the unknown. If we do not know what is going to happen, we feel out of control. We equate giving up control with being powerless. When faced with change, and the fears it naturally engenders within us, it may be helpful to remember that it is impossible to achieve a higher vibrational status *without* change.

Souls that have chosen this area of mastery generally do everything possible to keep everything in their life on an even keel. They believe that in order to succeed they need to keep everything just the way it is, under their control, unchanging. They often tend to attract teachers who think just the same way they do. These are also people who have a difficult time balancing their hearts and their heads. They tend to *think* instead of *feel*, rationalizing every bit of information before making any decisions. In fact, they often have a very hard time making any decisions at all. This particular attribute can be very deceptive because it does not always appear to be a hindrance. Quite often, it is not until these people are faced with drastic change that they realize they are totally unprepared and unequipped for it. The paradox is, the comfort they seek is often best served by becoming comfortable with the process of change itself.

Case History No. 3

Name: Jim
Age: 41
Marital Status: Married
Profession: Health Spa manager
Life Lesson: Adaptation
Catalyst: Natural father
Type: Energy Matrix

Jim grew up in a naval household, consequently his family was always moving. When he was thirteen, Jim's parents got divorced and his mother married another naval officer who was of a higher ranking than Jim's father. Being military men, Jim's father and his stepfather were both strong disciplinarians. Whereas Jim had been able to take this discipline from his own father, he refused to accept it from his stepfather. This was rather unfortunate as, being of a higher rank than Jim's natural father, his stepfather was accustomed to being obeyed without question.

As happens with a lot of young adolescents, Jim started to rebel. In his case perhaps, it was understandable. After all, here was a boy who had spent his entire life moving from one military base to another. Just when he was beginning to get comfortable with a new school, new area and new friends, he would be forced to move on and start all over again. This, coupled with the emotional and psychological trauma of his parent's divorce, made it very difficult for Jim to trust people enough to allow himself to open up to them. The older he got, the more afraid he became of commitment, which in turn affected his relationships with girls. By the time he was fifteen, Jim felt so cut off and lonely, he started hanging around with the wrong crowd and getting involved in underage drinking.

Pretty soon he wasn't just getting into trouble with his parents; he was getting into trouble with the law, too.

Things didn't really start changing for Jim until he took up bodybuilding at the age of eighteen. For the first time in his life he found something he was good at, and soon he was winning bodybuilding competitions, which in turn helped him to develop self-confidence and self-respect.

Jim got a job working at a health spa, but even though he loved his work, he still had problems getting along with people. This was Jim's blind spot and it started to cause real problems for him with his colleagues and superiors at work. That's where Jim was at when he first called me for a reading. One of the first things he told me was that he loved to start things, but didn't seem to have what it took to follow through. He would get bored, or be too easily distracted. It was beginning to affect his career prospects and he didn't know what to do about it. He didn't understand what was going on because he couldn't see the overview.

Fortunately, I was able to explain to Jim about energy matrixes and energy stamps, and show him how, throughout his entire life he had been dealing with the lesson of Adaptation and learning to go with the flow. This was fairly obvious to me from the way that nothing had ever been constant or secure in his life. The continual moves from one home to another, one school to another, even one father to another, were all about learning to become comfortable with adapting to change.

Once I'd been able to help Jim see the patterns that were at work in his life it wasn't difficult for him to see that he could turn this to his own advantage by finding ways to work with, rather than against, his energy matrix, and thus learn to master it.

Jim found the perfect job for himself. He now works as a project manager for a large chain of fitness clubs. He's in charge of establishing new locations. Once each new club is up and running he then moves on to the next one, so he doesn't get bored or have to deal with the parts that are repetitive and uninteresting for him.

It's been said that the definition of insanity is trying the same thing over and over again in the expectation that things will be different. While people working with Adaptation may understand this concept on an intellectual level, they are incapable of applying it to themselves. Thus, as strange as it may seem to the rest of us, many of them actually *do* keep on banging their heads against the same old walls, repeating the same old mistakes, and all the while expecting different results.

All humans have a resistance to change. We want to be comfortable, and by its very nature, change is anything but that. As difficult as change is for the rest of us, however, it is ten times as difficult for those working with the life lesson of Adaptation and change, as they typically have such a strong blind spot they cannot even see when they are uncomfortable with what's going on in their own life, and that's what makes them so resistant.

Jim is unusual in that he *is* learning to master his life lesson of Adaptation. Instead of trying to change things, which would be impossible anyway, since in his case it is an energy matrix and not an energy stamp, Jim is learning to see the gift in this life lesson and make it work for him, rather than continuing to resist and rebel against it.

Now if this has been an energy stamp, there are various therapies Jim could have tried to help him overcome some of the behavioral patterns that had resulted from the constant disruption he'd suffered as a young child and adolescent. Neuro-linguistic programming (NLP) is one of them. Hypnotherapy is another. But since this was an energy matrix, none of these things would have worked because an energy matrix cannot be changed, it can only be mastered.

Case History No. 4

Name: Maryann
Age: 34
Marital Status: Recently Engaged
Profession: Social Worker
Life Lesson: Adaptation
Catalyst: Father
Type: Energy Stamp

Maryann first came to me after reading one of my books. She saw the potential for a different, more open kind of life than the one she was presently living. Even though she really wanted to incorporate into her life some of the principles in the book, she simply could not see herself putting them into action. She was in a job she disliked, but had tolerated for ten of her thirty four years. The real reason for her call was evident in her first two questions. How difficult, she wanted to know, would it be for her to change? Could I give her a step-by-step method that would allow her to evaluate whether she would be able to transform her life? As she asked these questions, I clearly saw a connection to her father. When I asked about her early life with Dad, she said that she had very few childhood memories of her father. Since this is often indicative of childhood abuse issues, I asked her what other memories she had of her early childhood. She revealed that she had perfect memories of other events leading all the way back to three years of age. Since I was still sensing signs of emotional and physical abuse, I inquired about her relationship with her father today. She began to paint a picture of her relationship with Dad that led me to suspect that she was working with a life lesson of Adaptation.

Maryann's Mother had spent her entire married life trying to not upset her husband. She passed this attitude on to her children, who grew up with the idea that creating a successful home life meant keeping the peace at all costs. Maryann's Mother was clearly working with a life lesson of Definition and had substituted one master manipulator - her mother - for another, her husband. She had wanted her own children to have the loving, caring support that had been lacking in her own life. Instead, Maryann's mother had simply enabled her husband to rule the household with fear and intimidation.

Maryann's Mom was the key player in her life, yet Dad was clearly the catalyst. During our conversation Maryann suddenly had a memory resurface of an event involving her father that had occurred when she was four. She thought it was quite odd that this memory should surface now, in reality it happens all the time in my private sessions. Maryann had been teaching her two-year-old brother to sing. To her parents, it sounded like they were having a screeching contest. Mom called from the kitchen, telling the kids to tone it down as they did not want to upset their father. Maryann recalled hearing her father stomp into the kitchen. Her voice quivered as she remembered hearing a horrid sound. Her mother had then quietly slipped into the bathroom. Maryann had followed, and on seeing her mother's bloody mouth had instantly known that her father was responsible for her mother's tears and pain. On entering the bedroom she then saw her Father quietly sobbing on the bed. While Maryann's Dad clearly had an anger problem, it had never erupted in this fashion before. As it happened, it never erupted in violence again. But it was enough to imprint Maryann with the energy stamp. From that day forward Maryann's relationship with her

Father was based on keeping the peace in order to prevent a further violent reaction.

As much as Maryann wanted a relationship and children of her own, the fact that she had spent her entire life walking on eggshells, trying not to rock the boat, prevented her from realizing her dream.

Meanwhile, Maryann's Dad, who was working on a primary life lesson of Trust, was motivated to learn to deal with his anger. The tragedy was that with a secondary life lesson of Communication, no one knew that Maryann's Dad had dealt with his anger, so everyone continued behaving in the same vein. The interesting part of this is that though Maryann had never actually been abused, she carried the energy stamp of abuse just the same. This is a perfect example of what I call a transferred energy stamp, in which an energy stamp gets transferred from one person to another simply by being in the energy field, without undergoing the actual experience itself.

Here, I used a technique that I have found to be very successful. I simply asked Maryann to imagine herself as a neutral observer of her own life. This allowed her to remove any emotional attachment to these events, release any judgments and simply view the situation as if it were happening to someone else. I then showed her the larger perspective that I was seeing as contracts she had made to facilitate her own life lesson. Although she thought this was interesting she could not relate it to her situation. Nonetheless, the seeds had been planted. About four months later she called for another session. This time she asked a lot of questions about what had occurred in the previous session. Even though I remembered very little of our previous conversation I was immediately able to see the exact same scenario that I had described before. Suddenly Maryann got a glimpse of the larger picture and wanted to know where to go from here. Now Maryann was open to the knowledge that she was working on a primary life lesson of Adaptation. Since she was no longer afraid of her Father, I suggested that she could begin to heal this energy stamp by taking him out to lunch and speaking to him of the event that had occurred when she was four years old.

Three weeks later I received a very lengthy and excited message on my answering machine. Maryann had brought everything out into the open with her father and had learned that the event she had recalled so vividly had had two distinctly opposite effects. For her, it had been the catalyst that had taught her that there was safety in maintaining the status quo. For him, the lesson had been there was danger in maintaining the status quo, and thus it had provided him with a reason to change. Of course, with Communication as a secondary life lesson he had never said anything to make anyone see that he had changed.

Maryann's father had thought she had been far too young to remember, and was even surprised to find it had created such an impact on her life. The real high point for Maryann was that her father had apologized for this incident and for not being there emotionally for her as she had grown up. The tears they shared that day healed both of them. Not only did they begin a new relationship based on communication, it also gave Maryann the confidence to start seeking change.

The last time I spoke to Maryann she told me she was now in a relationship, that she had moved home twice, and that she had changed her job. She is now working with children and she loves her work. For someone who had built her life completely on a foundation of always keeping things the same, Maryann was now taking more risks than she had ever envisioned and in the process was enjoying life more than she had ever dreamed possible.

Primary Life Lesson #3

Be-ing

Wholeness

W hen we first began the game it was necessary for us
to leave the first dimension of unity and travel through
the second dimension to land in the third. As we passed
through the second dimension we acquired a field of
polarity. This is where we separated ourselves into the
sexes and started seeing things as separate from one
another when, in fact, every single thing that exists is an
integral part of everything else.

The illusions of the field of polarity in which we still reside
conspire to make us believe that we are not whole. People
who choose a life lesson of Be-ing have an especially
difficult time with this.

Like all life lessons, this too can be facilitated either by an
energy matrix or an energy stamp. Those who choose an
energy matrix to facilitate this life lesson spend a lot of time
looking for external things to add to themselves or their
lives in order to make themselves feel whole.

In some instances these are people who feel they must
find something, or take something, or add something
to themselves in some way in order to enhance their
mood. Some people in this situation use food to make
themselves feel safe. Others may become obsessed with
self-enhancement, i.e., making themselves look prettier or
'better' in some way. Still others become 'study junkies', in
the belief that acquiring credentials will make them all they
wish to be.

Whatever they choose, it can easily – and, in fact, often

does – turn into an obsession or an addiction. Obsessions, addictions and compulsive behaviors generally present the perfect opportunities for mastery of this Life Attribute.

Addictions

The Primary Life Lesson of Be-ing many times leads to addictions. In the case of any addictive behavior, it can be very helpful to first identify whether the life lesson is being facilitated by an energy matrix or an energy stamp. So often a healer attempts to heal an energy matrix rather than finding ways to master it. (See the chapter on Energy Stamps - Energy Matrix.) This can be very frustrating for both the healer and the client. The life lesson of Be-ing lends itself well to addictions. Since the main pattern of this life lesson is that people look outside of themselves for things to make them whole, it is easy to see how this attribute can easily turn into a reliance and even addiction upon the things they think will make them whole. This does not mean that every addictive person has a Primary Life Lesson of Be-ing, however addictive behavior is often precipitated by this life lesson.

Leaning Relationships

In the case of those who are constantly seeking to find wholeness through their relationships, this often results in a 'leaning relationship'. Leaning relationships are those in which two people lean on one another, both believing that neither of them is whole on their own, and thus can only become whole by having the other to complete them. The problem is that it's virtually impossible for two people to grow at exactly the same rate, so it's only a matter of time before one person grows and the other, inevitably, falls.

Master Manipulators

There are situations in which people have become so badly injured that they spend much of their life in self-defense mode. A person who has chosen to combine several lessons in one experience may find themselves being severely emotionally wounded at a very early age. Sometimes these dear souls build walls around their hearts and then expend a great deal of their energy manipulating other people from behind those walls. As they grow into adulthood they can become what I term a 'master manipulator.' Of course, this is rarely done intentionally or even consciously. The problem is, they get so good at it they are not even aware they are doing it. Frequently, the people they tend to attract into their life to subconsciously 'manipulate' are those who have poorly defined boundaries.

Weight Problems
Are you fat? This may sound like a strange question, but I have found that it's often those with the biggest and most loving hearts who are battling with weight problems. In many cases, these people find it almost impossible to see their own beauty. If you are one such person, here's a perfect opportunity to view your situation in a different light. First ask yourself, is your extra weight the result of an energy stamp or an energy matrix? If it is from an energy stamp, ie; something you learned or acquired due to your life experiences, remember those experiences can be healed, and when they are, your weight will automatically change.

If your weight issues are the result of an energy matrix, however, you could stop eating all together and *still* find that you may keep putting on weight. This is because an energy matrix cannot be changed, it can only be mastered. The lesson here is to first learn to see yourself in a completely different light – i.e., as being whole and complete just the way you are at this very moment, and to learn to bless and to love your body.

If you search for the key to mastery and find all the gifts that this energy matrix is affording you, and then learn to use these gifts to their fullest, I guarantee you *will* see a difference. The very first difference you'll see is that your weight will become less important to you. When that happens, your body will finally be free to adjust itself.

I facilitate people with this life lesson by encouraging them to find the sacred space within, where they can simply *be*, instead of always trying to be something, or someone, they are not. Find the place where you can learn to appreciate what you already *are* and just *be* with that. The art of simply Be-ing is foreign to most of us, but with practice they will see real change, first in their energy field and then in their life.

From Be-ing into Truth

The life lesson of Be-ing often precedes the life lesson of Truth. The experience gathered in a life that requires one to master the Lesson of Be-ing can easily set the stage for a life lesson of Truth to follow. People working with a life lesson of Truth will always be looking for someone else's truth, or the latest and greatest truth, or the newest concept, etc. That's a bit different from this life lesson, however, because that life lesson relates *specifically* to Truth, whereas this life lesson relates to the entire being. Thus, it's about always looking for what you think is missing within you.

Case History No. 5

Name: George
Age: 45
Marital Status: Widowed
Profession: Incarcerated
Life Lesson: Be-ing
Catalyst: Father
Type: Energy Matrix

Growing up, George wanted nothing more than for Albert, his father, to acknowledge how proud he was of his son. George desperately needed to hear his dad say, "I see who you are, son, and I love you." But it never happened. It wasn't that Albert wasn't proud of George, or didn't love him; it's just that he was working with a life lesson of Communication, and thus was incapable of speaking the words George yearned to hear. So instead of telling George how he really felt, Albert would say things like, "If only you were *this* way, you'd be better..." Or, "If only you'd studied more in school... or were better behaved..." etc. What he really meant was, life would be a whole lot easier for George if he were to approach things in a different way. But owing to his own difficulty with words, Albert could never express himself properly. The result was, George became imprinted with the energy stamp of believing that he is 'not enough,' and thus will always need 'something else' in order to make him better than he is.

On one level, George did sense that his father really loved and cared for him. But instead of making things better for George, this only made them worse because he just couldn't understand why his father could not bring himself to say the words. All George wanted was for Albert to validate what George believed at heart. George was convinced that if he could only get his father to admit that he accepted and loved him unconditionally, just as he was, George would be able to start feeling good about himself, instead of feeling inadequate and less than whole. Sadly, because that validation was never forthcoming, George spent his entire life always seeking things outside of himself to make him feel complete.

As he grew into manhood, George developed a reputation as someone who would do the most inappropriate things to get attention. He got involved with drugs, and started taking all kinds of stupid shortcuts that usually landed him in trouble of one kind or another. Some of the things he did were so incredibly dumb that, to outsiders, it looked as though George wanted to get caught. Finally, one night, George flipped. He got into an argument with his wife, things escalated into violence, and George ended up killing her and dumping her body. As if that weren't bad enough, he just happened to choose a place that had cameras that caught his every action. Of course, the whole thing was caught on film and George ended up with life imprisonment for murder.

Now if George could only have healed this energy stamp by either accepting what he intuitively knew or at least sharing his feelings with his father directly, things could have turned out differently.   Instead, he kept it all inside and allowed the resentment to build. The result was he not only killed the wife he loved, but he also ruined his own life. As far as I know, he is still directing his anger at his father.

What makes this particular case so interesting, as well as poignant, is that Albert was also my client, so I got to see this story from a completely different perspective, as you will learn when we get to the section that deals with the life lesson of Communication.

Case History No. 6
Name: Steve Rother
Age: 53
Marital Status: Married
Profession: Author
Life Lesson: Be-ing
Catalyst: Father
Type: Energy Matrix

This book would not be complete without the personal stories and case histories to show how this material applies in real life. Since I share the stories of others so freely I think it's only appropriate to share my own primary life lesson. When the Group was showing me this information I naturally attempted to apply it to my own life experience first. As I explained earlier, I first saw a little bit of myself in all of the primary life lessons. However, when I detached and looked at my life objectively I did, in fact, see patterns that indicated a specific life lesson. My primary life lesson is Be-ing. As I look back, I can see that many of the positive and negative experiences I have had in my life all pointed in the same direction.

One of the biggest challenges I have had to work with was alcoholism. My recovery began in the 12-Step program more than 20 years ago. I have nothing but the very best to say about this program as it saved my life. I was well respected and somewhat of a father figure in these meetings over the many years. I set up new groups and sponsored dozens of people over the years. I considered this to be one of my great successes in life. In retrospect, I believe that it was the first opportunity for me to see myself as a healer. I still refer people to the program when the opportunity is right. However, even though I was able to use the negative challenge of alcoholism to help other people, and, therefore, to find mastery, still there was something missing. I mention this for several reasons. One is that I have always wondered why I was able to make this work in my life while so many friends and others I sponsored could not stay sober. No matter what they did, they inevitably fell back into the abyss. There were four people in particular that I will never forget. Three of them died from alcohol poisoning while I was working with them.

There was another enigma I became aware of which

added to my confusion. During this time I couldn't help noticing that a number of people who had been very successful at quitting drinking without the help of any programs, 12-step or otherwise. They simply quit all by themselves. There were also a number of others I knew in the program who, after remaining sober for a long period of time, were able to start drinking again in moderation, and keep things in check without any apparent problem. According to the 12-step program, this was not something that should ever happen, yet the evidence clearly suggested otherwise. These anomalies bothered me as I had no reference for them.

When the Group started working with me I began to pull away from it all. I still believe in AA and the 12-steps program as a way to shift the energy because, quite simply, it works. But when the Group started communicating with me several years ago I began to have a problem with the general belief in personal powerlessness that such system seemed to promote. Week after week, I saw the same people coming in, relating the same stories. Beyond giving up drinking, few seemed interested in moving forward or advancing their lives in any way. Everything was 'taken easy' and very few people seemed to support the motion of pursuing one's individual passion and joy. This began to be a problem for me, as the message of personal empowerment, which made such sense to me, did not seem to be one that was widely accepted at the meetings I attended.

It was about this time that I started seeking answers from the Group to some of the bigger questions I had, like, why did the 12-step program work for some people and not for others? And why is it that some people are able to quit their addictions without any outside support or help? That was when the Group started showing me the workings of energy matrices and energy stamps.

If you remember, an energy matrix is something we are born with. As such, it is 'hard-wired' in our system and therefore can not be healed or changed, it can only be mastered. An energy stamp, on the other hand, is something that gets 'imprinted' upon us, either as a result of an experience or event that may occur, or as the result of constantly being in someone else's energy.

With this fresh perspective I began to look more carefully at the dis-ease of alcoholism. I began to see that those who were able to quit drinking on their own, as well as those who, once they had beaten their addiction, seemed to be able to resume drinking again in moderation without any apparent danger of becoming alcoholic had chosen to facilitate this life lesson through the means of an energy stamp. Once the stamp was healed their reality changed. Now I understood why will power and other forms of traditional healing did not always work. In the case of an energy matrix, there is nothing wrong and thus there is nothing to be healed. It is simply the way some people, including me, are wired – i.e., we have addictive wiring.

In the Be-ing life lesson we have an innate belief that we are not whole and, therefore, need to add something to ourselves in order to become so. The key here is not powerlessness, but rather lies in understanding that the addiction can be transferred. In fact, it is my opinion that the reason the 12-step program worked so well for me was because I simply transferred my addiction from alcohol to the program itself.

Nowadays, I simply allow myself to be addicted to things that do not harm me. The overwhelming attraction I once had to alcohol is now focused on Lightwork. Sometimes I cannot wait to get up in the morning because I so love what I do. I travel all over the world connecting family and giving hugs and proudly call myself a professional Hugger!

Today I choose not to drink. It's really not a big deal for me anymore. With more than twenty years of reinforcement and sobriety behind me, I can honestly say that I no longer have any interest in alcohol. I simply have too much passion for my work, and too much to do to drink. The energy associated with drinking is simply not worth any of its 'benefits.'

Interestingly, I have since had many well meaning people, including several teachers in the new energy, tell me that now that I have been healed I can drink normally again. I know they mean well, but as a healer myself I firmly believe that it is no longer appropriate to try to take people's power away from them in that fashion. In the new paradigm of facilitation only the client can make those decisions. The healer's job is merely to create the space for them to do so. The truth is, I now know that having an addictive nature is my energy matrix and instead of fighting against it or trying to change this fact. . . I am *choosing* to master it.

Primary Life Lesson #4

Charity

Harmony

As we evolve as individuals, we go through phases, taking on lessons that relate to each other in some way. Since we also go through different phases as a collective, it's not uncommon for certain life lessons to become popular at different periods in time. Right now, the life attribute of Charity is not popular in our society. That does not mean it is not important, however. On the contrary, the life lesson of Charity holds the key to our next level of advancement as we progress toward becoming Human Angels.

The lesson of 'Definition' or 'centering one's own energy' would appear to be somewhat in contrast to the lesson of Charity. But once our energy is centered to the degree that we can function well, it then becomes essential for us to reach out to others. Thus, both these attributes, Charity and Definition, can coexist and be employed simultaneously in one lifetime.

As we become more evolved, we are becoming more unity conscious. Our fascination with the search for extraterrestrial life shows that our hearts recognize a fundamental truth, which is that we are not alone. We all are an integral part of each other and what each of us does has an effect on everyone else on Earth, as well as beyond.

The word Charity has become synonymous in our society with 'giving.' However, although this can be one expression of Charity, true Charity is not just the art of giving alone. Our governments are learning very quickly that giving, by itself, only results in creating dependencies that feed on themselves, thereby breeding further dependencies. True Charity, in terms of a life attribute, means honoring the connection we have to all people, and practicing this in all our actions. When our actions honor all people we are the ones who rise. In order to apply Charity, however, we must first learn to center our own energy.

Depending on where a person focuses these attributes this lesson can appear very differently. With these attributes focused inward we see people working with a life lessons of Charity appearing to be selfish and self-serving. With the lack of connection they focus inward as if no matter what they try, they simply can't get their own needs met. In the lower levels of mastery their own needs and feelings are foremost because their disconnection to those around them means they simply can't feel much else. This makes them appear to others as inconsiderate. The dichotomy is that it is only possible to feel whole when we make connections to others, yet, it is extremely difficult and awkward for them to do so. While many in this situation have already mastered the attribute of Definition (see the Primary Life Lesson of Definition), they have not yet learned to apply it to others, because with this disconnection they haven't learned to relate to those outside of themselves. Although it will seem to them that they became this way as a means of survival, their task is to learn to understand their true connection to those around them.

On the other hand, if these attributes are focused outwardly, in the lower levels of mastery this will appear as a person who over-compensates in relationships. They may appear to be in your face demanding to be the center of your attention. They often appear as the person who tries too hard to be liked. They don't have the feedback from people around them so they don't know when to quit.

Their inner belief is that they will have what they need if everyone likes them. It is here that they over-compensate and quite often unintentionally alienate themselves. These people have the ability to drain others around them. As they master this life lesson they will find that it is through honoring this connection not by trying to make everyone love them but by learning to feel the connection.

Please keep in mind that, as I have described the above examples in the lowest levels of mastery. I have purposely done this for the simple reason that it is much easier to see these attributes in their most difficult state. As a person works with this life lesson they learn to master it in stages and, therefore, you will varying stages of these attributes. Mastering the attribute of Charity lies in strengthening the connection that already exists between all things around us.

Case History No. 7

Name: Phillipe
Age: 55
Marital Status: Single
Profession: Engineer
Life Lesson: Charity
Catalyst: Mother
Type: Energy Stamp

Phillipe is a French electronics engineer who is working with the life lesson of Charity. He lives alone and has very little connection to people around him. Whereas people working with the life lesson of Definition usually are hugely sensitive and almost afraid to say things to others because of the reaction their words might elicit, Phillipe appears to be totally impervious to other people's feelings and reactions, and only interested in his own feelings.

Consequently, most people who know or meet Phillipe dismiss him as being someone who is totally crass, self-centered, or selfish – and often all three.

Now, obviously, I have to be careful when counseling people like Phillipe. I cannot just say outright that their behavior is selfish and inconsiderate. I have to be diplomatic and sensitive to their feelings. So instead of telling them that they are disconnected from others – which they would have no frame of reference for anyway, I usually approach the subject more subtly. In this particular case, I simply said to Phillipe, 'What I'm seeing here is that other people perceive you as being selfish. Is that correct?' He seemed really surprised that I had 'hit the nail on the head' so accurately and immediately responded by saying, 'You're absolutely right. How on earth did you know that?'

Having started out by showing Phillipe quite clearly that I was seeing who he really is, I was then able to start talking to him gently about his blind spot – i.e., not being able to register any connection to other people.

"What I'm seeing here," I told him, "is that you were an extremely sensitive child. But this worried your mother so much that, out of fear that your feelings would be trampled upon and hurt, she did everything she could to toughen you up and make you less sensitive." This was understandable to a degree. Phillipe's mother had lived through some very difficult times during the Second World War. Her primary motivation was to protect her son and ensure he became capable of taking care of himself in the event that anything should happen to her. So she deliberately set out to '
"make a man of him."

Throughout Phillipe's childhood she was always admonishing him to "stiffen up," "to stand up for himself and be a man." Without realizing it, Phillipe's mother taught him to be selfish and always put himself first.

Now Phillipe wasn't very happy with the neighbors who shared the duplex building he lived in. As far as he was concerned, they were noisy and inconsiderate, because they dared to walk around their home at nighttime with their shoes on. On several occasions he had knocked on their door and bluntly told them to have more consideration and take their shoes off when they were indoors. Well, of course, as far as the neighbors were concerned, Phillipe was just a rude and grumpy old man who only cared about himself. And of course they were right. But it wasn't really Phillipe's fault. His mother had more or less overwritten all trace of his former sensitivity by imprinting him with such a strong message of selfishness.

Once we talked about his mother and some of the awful things she had lived through, like being forced to witness her own mother's murder, Phillipe began to understand why he was the way he was, and why his mother had behaved as she had. Given what she had lived through, she had every right to be scared.

By offering Phillipe my perspective, I was able to remove the judgment, both good and bad, of his mother's behavior. At the same time this also allowed me to gently show him how his mother had merely been the catalyst for the life lesson of Charity that he had set up for himself.

By the end of our 45-minute session I had helped Phillipe trace back to their point of origin many things he had never been able to comprehend. At first, he had some difficulty understanding why I was talking about his mother and his childhood when his problem was with his neighbors. But once he started connecting the dots, it slowly began to dawn on him that there was a pattern here that needed to be looked at. In fact, I even asked him that question outright. "Is this something that seems to be a recurring theme in your life?" When he admitted it was, I told him, "this is what we call a blind spot."

After explaining to him about life lessons, I told Phillipe that the key to healing this energy stamp lay in finding a healthy balance between being considerate of his own needs and being sensitive to others'. We don't want to be too over-sensitive, but at the same time, it's important that we feel connected to those around us, as this is the beginning of unity consciousness.

Once he began to grasp what I was saying, I asked him how he thought his neighbors felt when he kept complaining about their behavior.

"They probably think I'm a jerk," he said, somewhat ruefully.

"So what do you think you can do to start changing their impression of you and build bridges between you?" I prompted.

"Well, I guess I could learn to word things a little differently," he suggested.

Had he ever thought of inviting his neighbor over for tea, or taking her a basket of flowers? I asked.

"No. I just thought about moving," he admitted candidly.

After spending a little more time talking about life lessons in general, and blind spots in particular, I was able to encourage Phillipe to put himself at a higher level of awareness and see how these patterns kept recurring throughout his life, and why. He was then able to see how he had set it all up for himself so perfectly. He'd even chosen a job in which it was helpful to be disconnected from people, since he often had to make harsh decisions. Had he been a more sensitive person, this could have been very difficult for him. As it was, his imprint made it easier for him to perform the more unpleasant parts of his job than it would have been for someone else.

On the one hand, one could almost say that Phillipe's job was helping him to master his life lesson, but personally, I think it had been hindering him.

A year went by before I heard from Phillipe again. He attended one of my seminars. The moment I saw him, I knew things had changed for him. There he was, sitting in the front of the audience, with a big beaming smile on his face. The moment the seminar was over, he couldn't wait to tell me that his whole perception of life was gradually changing. It wasn't always easy for him, but he was determined to do things differently.

The biggest key to understanding, he admitted, was when I had asked him to look at recurring patterns and used the words 'blind spot.' He still had a lot of work to, but he was slowly getting there. He'd finally learned to stop and take the time and effort to put himself in other people's shoes, as well as get in touch with his own feelings, before he spoke. Though the mother of his neighbor still disliked him, he'd made friends with her daughter and it no longer bothered him when she wore her shoes around the house.

The way I work when having a session with people is to encourage them to make their own connections by triggering insights with questions. I never try to take their power away from them. Instead, I will often say, "Let me tell you a story, because this is what I am seeing, and I'd like to know if it fits for you. And please feel free to interrupt as I really value the feedback." I'll describe what I am being shown by saying something like, "Was your mom this type of person?" Pretty soon, they start opening

158 - Spiritual Psychology

up and talking about their mother or father, and their childhood. Then I'll change the subject by encouraging them to talk about their job, and suddenly I can see all the patterns really clearly. Suddenly they are saying, "Yeah, yeah. It all makes sense now."   This is what typically happens when people consult me for a private session.

Case History No. 8

Name: Greta
Age: 67
Marital Status: Divorced
Profession: Retired
Life Lesson: Charity
Catalyst: Mother
Type: Energy Matrix

Greta is a lady with a huge heart. A retired beautician, she prides herself on her open-heartedness, and the fact that she loves everybody and she thinks everybody lives her. In social settings she is always at the center of attention and they one who takes to everyone. She has a rather large ego, which is okay, because she knows it, but she also has some sharp edges, and people only see the sharp edges because, with Charity as an energy matrix, she naturally has a blind spot when it comes to what other people feel about her.

Greta was born this way, which is to say she came in with this type of personality. Her mother was one of the best loved people on the planet. Greta was just 22 when her mother died, and literally hundreds of people turned up for the funeral. Greta's mom had been someone who had been able to give total unconditional love to others, and people went out of their way to return that love. She was a very rare and special lady. This meant, however, that Greta grew up in her mother's shadow. She always measured herself by how people felt about her and how many friends she had.

Once her mother had gone, Greta tried to step into her shoes. But because she was born with an energy matrix of Charity, she actually experienced quite a lot of difficulty living in harmony with people.

Greta's mother had never been able to understand why Greta appeared to rub people the wrong way. She'd recognized that her daughter was trying so hard that she over compensated and ended up pushing people away. Greta's mother was too close to her to be objective so she couldn't really help her much. In fact she was aware that her ease in relationships with other people actually made it more difficult for Greta as she measured herself against her. At the same time, because she had this blind spot where others were concerned, Greta could not understand why her attempts to emulate her mother and use her as a role model did not produce quite the same results in her own life. Somehow, no matter what Greta did or tried, nothing seemed to quite fit.

As a young girl Greta got involved in every social group she could, and did everything possible to be 'cool.' Although she prided herself on her popularity, what she didn't know was that when her back was turned, the other kids made fun of her and called her 'OG,' which was a cruel code name for "'bnoxious Greta."

She used to be fond of saying that she would go out of her way to love everybody, but when you were talking to her, you couldn't help feeling that she was really talking to herself, and not really connecting with anyone else on a meaningful level. So, despite all her grand displays and words to the contrary, Greta's behavior and body language were not congruent. People found her spiky energy a little harsh, and because it also was not difficult to deduce that her words and her actions did not match, people found it difficult to trust Greta completely.

Greta was married once – no one knows exactly what happened. All she will say on the subject is: "I threw that bum out." Whatever happened must have hurt her very deeply and contributed to her defensiveness. Although she has worked hard over the years to overcome her difficulties in relating to others, she still hasn't managed to attract a permanent partner, which is something she dearly wants in her life. The problem is, her outward behavior and attitude prevent men from 'seeing' who she really is behind the mask. Thus, they invariably tend to dismiss her as being too tactless, too direct, and far too lacking in diplomacy. And while she has softened somewhat in recent years, sadly, Greta still hasn't realized that it is she – and not others – who has the blind spot in this area.

As with most life lessons, one of the simplest ways to master an energy matrix like this would be for Greta to either write about her weaknesses, or simply open up and talk frankly about them to people. After identifying her life lesson and explaining the attributes to her she agreed that it was a fit. Then I asked if she really wanted to change it and she said she was really tired of this and she would do what ever it took. At this point I suggested to her that she begin with her closest and most trusted friends. If she could bring herself to say something like, "I am aware that I have this effect on people and I really want to change it but I need your help. I am now aware that I have a blind spot when it comes to seeing how I appear to others and I would like your honest feedback when you see me in these situations."

I heard from Greta a year later and although she was still struggling with this life lesson, the decision to do this was one of the most life changing events in her life. The interesting part is that for the first time ever people who knew her mother started telling her that she was just like her mom.

Primary Life Lesson #5

Communication

From the Heart

The Lesson of Communication from the Heart is defined within the sphere of relationships. Although this can apply to relationships of all kinds, relationships of love are the primary area in which we choose to work on this life lesson. However, it must be said that mastery of this particular life lesson has eluded many people because the objective is not, as so many believe, to complete one's self with *another*, but rather, to learn to walk *alongside* another, and share your life together *without either of you leaning too much on the other*.

Sharing truth is the essence of what creates a good relationship. But in truth, there is only one relationship in the new energy, that is the relationship of You with You.

This life lesson is more commonly undertaken in male form. Quite often people working with a life lesson of Communication will have difficulty talking as a small child. They may have a speech impediment, or they may be slow to learn to speak. After overcoming such early challenges, many will choose to place themselves in situations where they have to communicate for a living. If they should make good progress in mastering this lesson they usually do quite well with communications. Even so, speaking what is in their hearts may always prove difficult or challenging, because voicing their feelings honestly and letting their needs be known is not easy for them. If this life lesson is being facilitated via an energy matrix they may be prone to retreating behind a wall of silence whenever they become tired or stressed. These are people who will stick their heads in the sand at every opportunity.

Even in cases where two lovers who have shared several previous lifetimes together are reunited, the key to mastering this attribute still lies in not assuming that words are not necessary to express their feelings.

The reason that most souls working on this attribute often elect to incarnate in the male gender is because it is men that generally experience the most difficulty expressing their feelings. For several thousand years, men in our society have had their emotions anesthetized. Thankfully, this is changing fairly swiftly now as the new energy filters in.

Emotions are the bridge between the energy matrix and our Energy Tubes. (See the chapter on Clearing your Energy Tubes.) Thus, all of the Primary Life Attributes that we are working on will trigger strong emotions within us. Whether it is the energy matrix or the energy stamp that is the chosen vehicle of facilitation, both will be played out through our emotions. Because of this, mastering the attribute of Communicating from the Heart is one of the Primary Life Attributes that helps to facilitate all the others.

As we learn to master the art of always saying what we feel, the attribute of communicating from the heart will become the foundation of every relationship.

Case History No. 9

Name: Albert
Age: 82
Marital Status: Widowed
Profession: Retired
Life Lesson: Communication
Catalyst: Father
Type: Energy Matrix

Albert is the father of George, whom you may remember was the subject of one of the case studies presented earlier in the section on the life lesson of Be-ing.

Albert grew up with a severe stammer, so right from the beginning he had difficulty putting his thoughts and feelings into words. It didn't help matters that his own father used to get impatient with him, saying things like, 'Spit it out, boy,' or, 'Come on, get it out and just say what you mean.'

There was a lot of love in Albert's family, and his parents were good people. Even so, these interactions and dynamics, which remained largely unconscious, were necessary to provide him with the perfect setup for this life lesson.

So, here we have a person working with the life lesson of Communication who literally cannot speak what he feels, because he has real physical difficulties articulating his feelings. What happens, because we always learn to adapt and adjust to things, is that Albert learns to sidestep his disability by operating through his head and thinking everything through before giving voice to it. In the process, he learns to stifle all emotion, so that what comes out of his mouth is very specific, very precise and, of course, very controlled. Consequently, the hardest thing in the world for Albert to do is to say what he *feels*, as opposed to what he *thinks*.

We know, of course, the tragic effect that Albert's inability to speak what was in his heart had on his son, George. But when viewed purely from the perspective of the father, Albert's actually made excellent progress in mastering this life lesson. What he has learned to do is to consciously stop and let the energy flow through him without impedance. Instead of clamming up and operating through his brain, Albert has learned from his experience with George to allow himself to express his feelings of frustration about wanting to speak to George and yet, at the same time, also feeling that as long as he felt the emotion in his heart, he didn't have to express it in words.

In a sense, looking at this relationship from Albert's point of view, George's behavior, which was unwitting fueled by Albert's inability to express emotion, created the perfect situation for the father to learn to master this life lesson. When we look at this situation from George's side, however, things look altogether different.

Ironically, the older Albert gets, the more adept he is becoming at articulating the thoughts and feelings he could never express before. The last time I saw him, he didn't appear to have any problem telling his caregivers what his needs were, or articulating how he feels. But that's the way it often works. Sometimes we don't get it till the last minute, but when we get it, we get it. Now, that is mastery,

The other interesting thing about this particular case history is that Albert spent his entire career working in the communications industry. Here again, this is not as uncommon as one may think with our life lessons.

Case History No. 10

Name: Tony
Age: 35
Marital Status: Married,
Profession: Automotive Sales Executive
Life Lesson: Communication
Catalyst: Grandmother
Type: Energy Matrix

Tony is an intelligent young man. An sales executive for an auto dealer, Tony has chosen to place himself into a career situation in which his living is very much dependent upon his ability to communicate well for a living.

Tony prides himself not just on his "gift of the gab," but also on his ability to know what his customer is thinking. So not surprisingly, he considers himself to be an extremely good communicator. However, at the end of the day, Tony goes home to his wife and two kids, and none of them have a clue who this man really is, because Tony never opens himself up sufficiently to allow even those closest to him to see what is in his heart.

Just like Albert did in his younger days, Tony communicates entirely through his head. Despite his tremendous success at work, and his wonderful ability at fostering trust in his customers, when it comes to letting people see who he really is at heart, Tony has to *think* the process through and consequently ends up negating what he is feeling by running it through his head instead. This is what can happen when a life lesson of Communication is facilitated through an energy matrix.

Since having some private sessions with me, Tony has been able to work on this. He first came to me because he had read my book, Re-member, and recognized himself in it. Tony's marriage had always been somewhat rocky. He and his wife had broken up twice. When he started reading my book, it seemed to make a lot of sense to him. Because he recognized himself as having a lot of the same attributes as me, he not only felt that he could relate to me on a personal level, he also felt my story made sense of his own life.

When he called me to schedule a private session, I'm almost certain he was expecting to have some psychic tell his fortune for him. Right from the very beginning, it was fairly obvious to me that he was working with a life lesson of Communication. He told me he had never done anything like this before, and then immediately started telling me what he *thinks* about a number of things. When I asked him to tell me what he *feels*, all he could say was, "Well, I *think* I feel x..." and "I *feel* like I think y... And then I read your book and now I just don't know what to think."

"So why don't you tell me how you *feel*," I said, to which he replied, "I don't know what I feel... I just feel confused."

"Then tell me about your dad," I encouraged him, knowing that if I could just get him to go back into the past and tell me something about his childhood, we would find the way forward.

Tony told me that his dad had been a good provider. He'd always been around, and he had loved his children.

"Did he ever *tell* you he loved you?" I asked.

"No." Tony said. The more I probed, the more obvious it became that Tony's father had also been working with a life lesson of Communication. All through high school Tony had found that people misunderstood him. Because he had problems communicating from the heart, people were apt to misconstrue the things he said and the way he responded as a sign that he was snobbish and standoffish. By the time he got to college, Tony had begun to develop a number of strategies to cover up his difficulty with communication, so it became less obvious to people.

Tony loved cars, and once he graduated he got a job as a car salesman. Because it was important for his career, he started reading books and manuals on ways to improve his communication skills, and as a result he became extremely successful. Now you might think that all these tools

Tony was developing would inevitably make him a good communicator, and so they did, but only at work. This was because all his communications were client-centered, and thus did not require him to reveal anything about himself. Nonetheless, Tony met a lovely young woman, got married and had children of his own. That's when the pattern started repeating itself. Though he didn't realize it at the time, Tony's children grew up with the same emptiness he did. Just like his dad before him, Tony was a good enough dad, but as far as his children were concerned, he was just someone who was there. He rarely said a great deal at home, so his children never really got to know very much about him.

When Tony read my book it triggered something deep inside him. The more we talked, the more Tony began to relax and open up, until eventually he felt safe enough to tell me that he and his wife were experiencing some difficulties in their marriage. When I asked whether he had talked to his wife about them, he replied, "No. I don't know what to say or where to start or even how she will take it."

When I asked him a few more questions about his parents' relationship, it became fairly evident that history was repeating itself all over again, bringing Tony face to face with his life lesson of Communication. Growing up, Tony had never witnessed any communication about or expressions of connection or love between his parents. And although he had since developed a number of tools to help him become a good communicator when dealing with his customers, he'd never learned how to open up to his wife or children and openly express his emotions and feelings.

"When was the last time you told your wife that you were scared?" I asked him. "When was the last time you told her what really excited you?"

"We-e-l-l, we don't really talk a lot," he admitted.

"Then it's time you started," I suggested, "because it is intimate communications like these that build relationships. Now I don't want you to go completely berserk here and frighten the life out of her, so what I am going to suggest is that you start slowly by slipping one thing into a conversation with her each day that has something to do with how you *feel* as opposed to what you *think*. Start out with something small. Tell her, 'I felt this today.' Just sneak it into the conversation. Get comfortable with using the words. If you can manage to tell her something every day that gives her some insight into your *feelings*, rather than your *thoughts*, pretty soon you'll find yourself communicating on a whole new level. It doesn't matter how trivial or meaningless it seems, the point is to start getting comfortable with confiding and sharing. That's where intimacy begins. We're not mind readers. We can't know what is going on in someone else's mind and heart if they don't share it with us. The more you can open up and let your wife in on how and what you feel, the more free she will feel to do the same, and the closer you'll find yourselves becoming."

Tony didn't say a lot at the time, but I could tell our conversation had made an impact on him. Six months later he called for a second session, and I was certain of it. Things were gradually changing. It wasn't easy for him, but he was doing the best he could, and making small but significant advances. By his third session, he was telling me that his relationship with his wife and children had changed entirely. Finally, Tony felt like a real family man. More importantly he no longer felt alone.

The life lesson of Communication invariably plays out in our more intimate, one to one love relationships. If it's not lovers, or husband and wife, it will be between two best friends. In this new energy, we will find that there there's more of a blending of male and female energy going on. This means that men, who have become unbalanced by being stuck too far in their masculine side, will find situations cropping up that force them to explore and get more comfortable with feminine energy, and the gentler, more feminine sides of their own nature, while those females who have become too entrenched in the feminine energy are having to move more toward the masculine sides of their nature in order to create the perfect balance. This is what Freud referred to as the *anima* and *animus*. It's the yin and the yang. None of us are all masculine or all feminine. We all have both within us, and the trick is to learn to find the perfect balance of expression.

Interestingly, someone who is working with this life lesson often attracts a partner who is working on the life lesson of Definition or Charity. What often happens in these situations is that if one person changes and the other refuses to change along with them, the relationship will fall apart. But if both partners are working on their individual life lessons, what typically happens is that they may pull apart for a while and then come back together again to build a new relationship within the same framework.

In the same way that we go through different stages as individuals growing up here on earth, so, too, do we go through different lives as different genders. With the life lesson of Communication, it's more common for us to choose to go through it as a male than as a female, because the way our society is currently set up, we are more likely to experience the kind of conditions that will facilitate difficulties with Communication.

Primary Life Lesson #7

Creation

Expressing Self Power

Living within a field of polarity we cannot see that we are creators, and, therefore, we alone hold the power of creation within our own thoughts. We all have this blind spot to a greater or lesser degree. But it is even more true of people working to master the life lesson of Creation, as not only are they often oblivious to their own creations; they also are blind to their own ability to create. Even though these people have tremendous abilities of creation they have great difficulty channeling this into practical creations in their own life.

Depending on how they set it up, people working with this life lesson can find themselves in several situations. For example, they may be an artist who works for months or years on a brilliant piece of work, and then when they have their first showing, are so shocked that someone actually wants to buy their work that they accept the very first offer they get. Or another may be a really bright secretary or assistant who does all the important work on a project and lets the boss take all the credit. They may also be the person who everyone knows has great creative abilities, and everything they touch is an effortless masterpiece, yet, they have never been able to make a living at anything steady. Their blind spot always keeps them from seeing their own creations or their creative ability. Even so they can often find themselves successfully teaching the creative arts.

In our society it is the male who has traditionally been supported to create, thus, many souls working on this life lesson choose to incarnate as females. Add to this the lack of self confidence that many women seem to have, and what we often end up with is wives who hide their own creations from their mates. Or, wives who create *through* their spouses, thereby giving the illusion that it is the spouse who is doing all the creating. In this situation the husband will often appear to extremely successful, while the wife will appear to be unable to support or create for herself. Remove this relationship, however, and it often transpires that the husband's 'successful' business or project starts to fail without any apparent cause. This is one of many popular scenarios for mastering the difficult life lesson of Creation.

A belief in lack, and also sometimes perfectionism, often provide the perfect excuse for these people to not even try to create for themselves.

The key to mastering this life lesson is to find the balance to personal power, which lies in RESPONSIBILITY. Finding a way to take more personal responsibility will increase an individual's sense of personal power, thereby helping him or her to master the life lesson of Creation.

Learning to hold our own power of Creation while in physical form is second only to Grace as the most difficult life lesson to master. The illusions of living within a field of polarity make it very difficult for us to see that we are actually creating our own reality in every single moment. Add to this the lack of self-worth that many of us suffer from and it's easy to see why we are blind to the greatest secret of the Universe, which is:

We are God.

Once we can learn to understand the simple meaning of these three magic words, we will begin to balance our own power with responsibility. When this happens, we will learn to master the Art of Creation very quickly.

Somewhere along the way we assumed the belief that to hold our own power as creators means that we cannot make mistakes. The truth is, we are *incapable* of making a mistake, for the simple reason that if we are unhappy with the reality we have created, all we have to do is claim responsibility for our creation, and then undo it and start again. All too often, we become so caught up in and obsessed by our need to make the 'perfect' choice that many opportunities completely passes us by.

Those who have Energy Matrices that facilitate this Lesson may find it difficult to even begin engaging their own creativity. Often, they become so overwhelmed with getting everything right, they fail to do anything at all. The problem begins when creative energy is stifled in this manner, it soon builds to a critical pressure. This creates a reversed flow of energy, which in turn can put the body under such stress that it ultimately becomes vulnerable to any number of ailments to which the individual may have a genetic predisposition.

A belief in lack is also something that those experiencing this life lesson often 'set up' for themselves as an aid to mastering this life attribute. In truth, the natural state of Heaven is abundance. There is no greater abundance than that which we experience when we are Home. Abundance is an excess of energy in any given situation. It is the opposite of lack. It is only the veil of forgetfulness we live behind that causes us to believe that we are finite in form and energy, when the truth is we are actually *in*finite in energy. When we accept that we are infinite in energy, abundance is no longer an issue. When we are so fully in the flow that we can tap into our creative energy at any given moment, we have no need of *anything*.*

Besides perfectionism, lack, and the life traits described

above, there are many other contracts that we set up to help us fulfill a life lesson of Creation. With the veil in place, it is hard to remember who we are. Thus, rarely do we have a sense of just *Be-ing* while in biology. This is why self-confidence issues are so pervasive among those working with this life lesson. Add to this situation any negative energy stamps from a misdirected parent or teacher who failed to support us during childhood, and we have the perfect conditions in which to learn to master the Lesson of Creation.

Those working with the life lesson of Creation will have very pronounced creative abilities, but they cannot always see it. A lot of these people have the ability to be successful, famous writers and authors, but they never let their creative expression out.

When we are repeatedly told that we cannot do something, and, in spite of that, do it successfully anyway, the feeling (emotion) of power becomes stamped on our Energy Tube, to be carried with us always. Every time we have an opportunity to take and hold our own power, this energy stamp will get called into action and thus become reinforced. The real challenge lies in learning to alter this energy stamp in a positive direction. For one thing, most of us are unaware that we can intentionally create positive energy stamps for ourselves.

For another, many of us are so afraid of making a wrong move that we make no moves at all. In other words, we become so afraid of falling that we never learn to stand.

The balance to personal power is RESPONSIBILITY. Thus, the key to mastering the life lesson of Creation lies in increasing our personal power by finding ways to take more personal responsibility.

To read more information on this important topic, see the chapter on "The Five Traditions of Abundance" in my book, Welcome Home ~ the New Planet Earth.

Case History No. 11

Name: Sarah
Age: 34
Marital Status: Divorced
Profession: Artist
Life Lesson: Creation
Catalyst: Mother
Type: Energy Matrix

When Sarah first consulted me she was married, but the marriage was having some difficulties. Sarah didn't want her marriage to break down. Not only did she have a huge fear of failure, but she also did not believe she would be able to cope on her own.

Although Sarah wasn't aware of it, I was shown that there was a good possibility of divorce. So, without actually telling her what I saw, I tried gently to encourage her to stand in her own power and believe in her own abilities of Creation. But all Sarah could think about was the awful prospect of failing at something, and how on earth she would ever be able to support herself financially if her fears did materialize. Being married gave Sarah a lot of things that she thought she would never be able to recreate on her own.

I started talking to Sarah about her passion, asking her questions about the things she did that made her heart sing. She told me that she really enjoyed 'dabbling in' art and writing, and sometimes singing, but that these activities were 'only hobbies,' certainly not something she could ever make a career out of. The picture I was getting while she was talking, however, showed me just the opposite. The truth was, Sarah was not only a brilliant artist and fantastic singer, she was also a very gifted writer.

When I described what I was seeing to her, however, she dismissed it immediately. It seemed quite preposterous to her that these three passions could amount to anything other than 'little hobbies.' Worse yet, she actually seemed to believe that, even if she was better than average in these areas (which she strongly refuted), it was only because her husband's wealth allowed her to devote more time to her hobbies than most people did. Clearly, in Sarah's mind, her creativity was totally dependent upon having her day-to-day monetary needs met.

Six months later, Sarah contacted me again. By this time, she had indeed separated from her husband and was now going through a divorce. As before, she was very preoccupied with her financial situation. Because she and her husband did not have any children, he felt no responsibility for supporting her financially. Thus, not only was she fearful about her ability to support herself, she was also worried that even if she did manage to find a job, she might not be able to afford to continue indulging her "little hobbies," which, even though she "wasn't very good at them," were nonetheless still very important to her.

On this occasion it felt appropriate to talk to Sarah about her life lesson and her blind spot, as I perceived them. I started by describing what I was seeing from her past, and explaining that the catalyst for this life lesson had been her mother.

Sarah's mom was a well-known screen star. A beautiful, talented, and very competitive woman, she had somehow managed to instill in her daughter the belief that, whatever Sarah did, it would never hold a candle to Mom's achievements. But the truth, as I saw it, was quite different. Sarah's gifts outshined her mother's by a long, long distance. But because she had a blind spot and, therefore, was incapable of seeing it, she was more likely to take on a job serving hamburgers at McDonald's than take a chance on making her living doing what she had been born to do. Sarah's blind spot ensured she was incapable of seeing that, far from being untalented, she was actually capable of creating every single thing she wanted, desired or needed in life. It's no exaggeration to say that Sarah was so multi-talented, she literally could have performed in a concert one night, exhibited her work at a top-flight art exhibition the next, and attended a party to celebrate her first book reaching the top spot on the New York Times Bestseller List the next night. That's how talented and creative she was.

As with many people working on a life lesson of creativity, however, Sarah's blind spot about her own abilities took on the form of perfectionism. Consequently, nothing she did was ever quite "good enough" in her eyes. Plus, in her perfectionism, she allowed herself to get so caught up in wanting to make the *right* decision, and do things in the perfect, proper order, that she was incapable of deciding which of her three passions she should pursue first. And that's really how Sarah managed (again, this behavior is always unconscious) to block everything for herself.

The biggest thing I was able to do for her was to ask her three questions:

"Who ever taught you how to make good mistakes?"

"Who ever loved you enough to let you fail, and in so doing learn from some of the best mistakes you could ever make?"

And, "What would it take for you to do that now?"

Sarah didn't want to hear me at first. She didn't have time for all that, she said, she needed to concentrate on earning a living for herself. But I wasn't about to let her off the hook so easily.

"Do you ever stop to think," I said, "that moving into your passion, expressing your God-given talents, and allowing yourself to be of the highest use to the universe that you can be, could open up the door to making a better living than you are making now?" I asked.

Though she still wasn't quite ready to believe that she could be successful making a career out of any one of her passions, or even all three, my comment did give her pause for thought. "W-e-l-l," she said hesitantly, "If I were to do anything like that, I'd have to start out slowly and build it up gradually. I couldn't possibly quit my job."

That was all I needed to hear. "So what would it take for you to feel comfortable enough to give yourself the time and space to create that?" I prompted. Sarah didn't answer that one, she was too busy thinking.

As it transpired, Sarah did eventually start making some progress in moving past her insecurities and blockages. And just as I had seen, she did start experiencing some success. But having chosen an energy matrix to facilitate this life lesson, she is never going to *feel* successful. Even if she had not had her mother as a catalyst, she would always have felt inadequate, because that's how she was wired to be, and nothing can ever heal or change that. The key to mastery here is for Sarah to understand that she is *always* going to have a blind spot about her own abilities. If she gets 300 people attending an exhibition of her work she is going to fret that she didn't get a thousand. If she can just learn to accept this and just get on and do things for the sheer joy of being in her passion and expressing herself through her creativity, she will do just fine. That's all it takes.

It's not difficult to spot someone working on a life lesson of creativity. In addition to their tremendous talent, the very blind spot that prevents them from accepting their own giftedness often leads them to sell themselves short. We've all met people like this, such as the artist who sells his works for a paltry sum to the first bidder, rather than hold out for better offers. Or the 'overworked assistant' who does all the behind-the-scenes work on a project and then lets their boss take the credit. These are the kinds of people who are often referred to as the "power behind the throne." They would never dare sit on the throne because they don't believe they deserve to, but in reality, no one has more right than they do because they are the ones who actually *created* the throne in the first place.

Case History No. 12

Name: Jeannie
Age: 52
Marital Status: Divorced
Profession: Currently a successful Ad Executive
Life Lesson: Creation
Catalyst: Aunt
Type: Energy Stamp

All her married life, Jeannie had lived in her husband's shadow. Like Sarah, she was actually a very talented and capable woman. Others could see it, but she couldn't. So she jogged along, quite content to play a supportive role in both her marriage and the family business, until her children got married and started living their own lives. That's when everything started to fall apart, or so it seemed. In reality, the picture I saw when Jeannie had her first private session with me showed that things stood a chance of finally coming together for Jeannie.

Turning 50 was a difficult time for Jeannie. With her children all grown up and leading lives of their own, it felt like nobody really needed her any more. She and her husband got along well enough, for a couple who had been married 28 years, but the reality was, there was very little closeness or communication between them. If they weren't having a conversation that revolved around their business, they rarely had much to say to one another.

By the time she reached 52, Jeannie was on the threshold of sinking into a deep depression. She felt totally unloved, unlovable, and totally useless. All she could see in front of her was the slippery slope to old age and senility. What was the point of it all? She kept asking herself. In an effort to find something to hold on to, Jeannie started looking for answers by attending seminars and reading metaphysical books. The more she awakened, the more she began to question the wisdom of staying married to her husband. He'd always been very controlling, having to be the one to make all the decisions. Although she'd made an equal contribution to their business, he never gave her any credit for it. On the contrary, in front of others he would often minimized her role in their success, talk down to her and generally treat her as though she was less intelligent, and had less knowledge about everything than he did. Inevitably, the more Jeannie learned, the more she began to step into her own power, the bigger the chasm grew between her and her husband. She moved out, moved back, and then moved out again, all within the space of a few months. Finally, they separated permanently and started divorce proceedings. And that's when their once successful business started gradually falling apart. Though neither of them had been willing to acknowledge it, Jeannie had always been the true power, the driving force behind their business. While she had never appeared to take a front line role, all the time she had been creating through her husband. In reality, all the best ideas that he had taken the credit for, had come from Jeannie. Now that she was no longer around, the truth became apparent.

Just like Sarah, Jeannie had always had a blind spot about

her own talent and creativity. This had been imprinted on her by her father who, working with a life lesson of Trust, had never learned to trust his own abilities. However, because she had chosen to facilitate this life lesson through an energy stamp, which can be healed, Jeannie was finally able to reach a point where she could step into her own power and accept full responsibility for her gifts and talents.

Jeannie has her own business now and both she and it are doing very well indeed. Once she stopped trying to please everyone else and began putting herself first, she really started to blossom. She had a lot of fun doing things just for the sheer joy of doing them, and before she knew it, she'd not only created a very successful business for herself, she also became something of a leading light at her local amateur dramatic society, writing, producing and performing in plays.

Primary Life Lesson #8

Definition

Expressing Individuality through Boundaries

This primary life lesson is particularly common with women at this time. Most people engaged in mastering this lesson tend to be healers with great emotional empathy. They tap into others' emotions, thought patterns and energy so easily and unconsciously they often do not even realize that it is *not* their own energy that they are feeling. Because of this, they invariably have some difficulty setting proper boundaries for themselves. Having weak boundaries, they often attract a series of master manipulators into their life. What usually happens is that when these souls leave or are removed from one overbearing relationship without mastering the attribute of Definition, they will unconsciously pull another into their field to help them facilitate their incomplete lesson.

Most often the catalyst for this life lesson appears in these people's lives during childhood. If the catalyst is a negative influence, it will threaten their boundaries so thoroughly and consistently they cannot help but discover that their primary challenge lies in creating strong boundaries for themselves. Because their boundaries are weak or nonexistent, the definition of self for these souls will also be weak or non-existent. If, on the other hand, the catalyst is a positive influence, the people working on this life lesson will be encouraged from an early age to set very clear boundaries for themselves.

The key to mastering this very popular but difficult life lesson lies in learning to place one's self first. This is not an easy thing to accomplish, particularly since society teaches us from an early age that it is wrong to be selfish. The fact is, despite society's efforts to persuade us otherwise, placing ourselves first in all areas is the most important of all. To treat ourselves in any other manner is a misdirection of our energy. Placing ourselves first means placing ourselves *before* our children, partner, parents, siblings, friends, and co-workers. If you find this a shocking concept, remember, there is a huge difference between those who are self*ish* and those who put self *first*. Granted, both are placing themselves first in the flow of energy, but the similarities cease there. In the case of the former, the intent is to fill one's self at the expense of everyone else. In the case of the latter, the intent is to fill one's self first *in order that one has even more* to give to others. The key to Mastering this life lesson of Definition lies in learning to define one's own boundaries and becoming accustomed to placing one's self first in all situations.

There is another aspect to this attribute. The reason many people engaged in this life lesson experience such difficulty defining their own boundaries is because they have no concept of where their own energy field ends and another's begins. The paradox is, this extreme sensitivity is precisely what makes these people such powerful healers. If they can learn to define their own energetic boundaries, they will also find that they can use this same sensitivity intentionally to tap into another's emotional energy field to facilitate healing. Those who master the life lesson of Definition are very powerful healers. And 'no' is the most powerful word they can learn to use.

Case History No. 13

Name: Ted
Age: 43
Marital Status: Single
Profession: Artist
Life Lesson: Definition
Catalyst: Mother
Type: Energy Matrix

Ted came in with extremely strong energy and very weak boundaries. Indeed his energy was so strong, that his mother actually felt somewhat threatened by him because of it. Right from the outset he seemed to have a strong sense of 'knowing,' which scared her. Ted's mom had been abused as a child, so she was very defensive and mistrustful of most people. Where other people built boundaries, Ted's mom built walls. And while she really did love her son, her fear and trust issues caused her to be very controlling. Ted's mom did everything for him, and because he had weak boundaries he never learned how or where to draw the line and say no to her. If he had a problem at school, she would simply take control of the situation by marching into his classroom and talking to his teacher. If he had a problem with another kid she would think nothing of having it out with the child's parents. She was the epitome of the protective mother. And she was also a master manipulator.

As Ted grew he became adept at tapping into his extreme sensitivity to produce the most amazing artwork. He could capture the shape and form of the human body in exquisite detail, and his work was much admired.

Ted never did learn to resolve his issues with his mother. Consequently, when he had his first serious relationship as an adult the dynamics were exactly the same. Ted had attracted and fallen in love with a man who was as manipulative as his mother. Though he was never consciously aware of it, of course, Ted had orchestrated the perfect set-ups to enable him to master the life lesson of Definition, including arranging a number of back-up plans that would slot into place in the event he should fail to master this lesson at the first, second, and possibly even third opportunity.

Ted did very well financially. He never had any problems finding buyers for his art and, consequently, was easily able to provide a lavish lifestyle for himself and his partner. Though life was not always totally harmonious, they managed to stay together for many years, until Ted discovered that throughout their relationship, the partner he had totally trusted had secretly been stealing from him. Ted was devastated. He couldn't understand why or how it had happened. Being the stronger one in the relationship, his partner had always been able to manipulate Ted into agreeing to whatever he wanted, so it wasn't as if he had ever lacked for anything. Ted could barely bring himself to believe it. Yet the facts spoke for themselves. His partner had manipulated and cheated him out of his entire life savings. And at the age of 43 Ted was deeply concerned that he would not have enough time to rebuild his retirement fund. Worse yet, Ted worried that he would never be able to trust his own judgment again.

When people have weak boundaries, as those working on the life lesson of Definition have, and they are also extremely sensitive, as Ted is, they're prone to picking up on everyone's energy and emotions and believing that what they are feeling is their own. A perfect example of this are the people who can walk into a restaurant, sit down at a table, find themselves getting angry without understanding why, and never know that the couple who'd occupied the table before them had just had an argument.

Definition is a major life lesson that's very common among lightworkers, particularly females. And as has already been mentioned, there's only way to master it, and that's to learn to put oneself first.

Ted took on far too much responsibility for his relationship with his partner. Because he had never been taught to put himself first, he had never learned where his own energy field ended and his partner's began. Consequently, it was very easy for both his mother and his partner to manipulate Ted emotionally and make him feel responsible for everything that happened in their lives. When I pointed this out to Ted, he was able to see the pattern. And because his experience with his partner (which he himself had set up, remember) had made such an enormous impact on him, chances were, after this, he would finally realize that if he wanted to protect himself in the future, he needed to learn where to draw the line and when it is appropriate to say no.

Case History No. 14

Name: Rachel
Age: 38
Marital Status: Divorced
Profession: Psychologist
Life Lesson: Definition
Catalyst: Mother
Type: Energy Stamp

Rachel was an extremely empathic individual. She only had to walk into a crowded place, such as an airport and within five minutes she would find herself totally overwhelmed by all the heightened emotions that are discharged in such a place. As a child, other kids would make fun of her for being a "cry baby." The truth was, Rachel could feel other children's pain, fear and frustrations so acutely that it would bring tears to her eyes. She literally would suffer from sensory overload.

Rachel had grown up in an abusive family. Her father ruled the roost, often with his fist. Her mother thought the best way to protect Rachel would be to teach her to be a good, quiet girl, and do whatever it took to please or appease Daddy, so he wouldn't get angry and take it out on the rest of the family. By bringing her daughter up to consider everyone's feelings and well being before her own, Rachel's mother served as the negative catalyst in her life. It wasn't intentional, but the message she instilled in her daughter was "life will be smoother if you put everyone else first and yourself last." And of course, good, sensitive child that she was, Rachel learned the lesson well and did exactly as she was taught.

Later on, when she became a young woman, Rachel thought that the way to take her power lay in getting married and having a home and family of her own. She was wrong. Though she had several boyfriends as a teenager, the only man who appealed to her enough to want to marry him turned out –not surprisingly – to be an extraordinary master manipulator.

By the time she called me for her first private session, Rachel was on her second marriage. When she hit 30 she had started to awaken. Her interest in spiritual matters and desire to become a healer caused so much friction between her and her husband, she eventually left him. The problem was, her second husband, whom she had met at a spiritual seminar, was just the same.

It's important to mention here that master manipulators come in all shapes and sizes. They are not all totally self-absorbed and only out for themselves in the way that Ted's partner was. On the contrary, many, like Rachel's mother, are warm and loving people who genuinely believe that it's okay to do what they do because their primary motivation is to protect themselves and their loved ones. All the same, it doesn't matter whether a person is intentionally controlling or simply misguided, manipulation is manipulation. No one has the right to influence another's behavior or take away their power by imposing their own wishes or belief systems on them. When I explained this to Rachel, she was able to see and accept that all her life, she had been giving her power away to a series of master manipulators, starting with her mother and ending up with her second husband.

Rachel knew in her heart that she was a powerful healer but she didn't know what to do with it. Although trained as a Reiki Master, she didn't practice as much as she would have liked to as her husband always complained about clients coming to their home. It was too disruptive to their home life. He and their daughter were her first priority, he said, besides which, it was too draining for her to be giving all her energy away to others... and so the emotional blackmail – i.e., manipulation - went on.

I told Rachel all about the life lesson of Definition, and how important it was for people working with this to fulfill their own needs first, rather than constantly putting themselves last. I explained that people like her mother and her second husband were not bad people, it's just the way their life lessons interacted with her own. The whole idea was for her to learn to stand in her energy, to learn to draw firm boundaries and be able to say, "this is mine, and this is yours. I won't stop being aware of your energy or empathizing with your emotions, but I won't take responsibility for your feelings." Once she got the message, it didn't take long for Rachel to start making some long overdue changes in her life. I told her that her family might not be too happy to begin with, but she shouldn't let that stop her. Their feelings were their feelings, and they were entitled to them. That didn't mean she had to mistake them for her own.

In fact, Rachel did subsequently send me an e-mail telling me how she was progressing.

"Of course, my whole family thinks I'm being very selfish," she wrote. "My daughter's not sure she likes the new me, and my husband keeps grumbling that I'm not the girl he married."

"Good." I wrote back. "That's a perfect sign you're on the right track."

Things got sticky for a while, as they often do when one person in a family starts defining their boundaries. The other family members are bound to find the changes difficult for a while, and it's not uncommon for them to start indulging in a variety of manipulative behaviors designed to restore the status quo. But Rachel stuck to her guns. She loved her husband and her daughter, but she also loved herself. She came to the realization that if they loved her as much as they professed to, they would want to see her happy and fulfilled. She wasn't just on this planet for their benefit. She was here to fulfill her own needs and desires, and if she did that everyone would benefit.

One of the hardest things for her husband to cope with, she told me in another communication, was that suddenly, men were finding her attractive. While she was secretly pleased with this, she was also somewhat bemused as to why this should be. After all, it wasn't as if she had lost any weight, or changed her looks or style of dress in any way.

"Don't worry, he'll get over it." I replied. "And if he doesn't, it's not your concern. And the reason other people are finding you so attractive all of a sudden, is because you have finally started defining who you are and what you stand for, which is something we all find attractive in another. As for your daughter, once she gets over the shock of you changing, I'll bet she'll tell you she actually prefers her new mom to her old mom. For in the final analysis, all kids really want is for their parents to be happy."

As it transpired, Rachel's husband didn't get over the shock of her change. A couple of years later, she did a session with me again and told me that she was now divorced. And while it had been tough at the beginning, she was now really happy with her life. She had a wonderful, close, loving relationship with her daughter, who treated her with more respect than she ever had in the past. She was also working full time as a healer, and was studying to be a psychologist, as she'd discovered that she could also heal people with her words. She was even dating again. What's more she was fully aware that most of the men she attracted – and was attracted to – still had a tendency to want to manipulate her, but that was okay, because she now knows that so long as she stands firm and sets her boundaries straight away, she rarely experiences any problems.

Primary Life Lesson #8

Integrity

Walking in Harmony with Self

Have you ever watched someone making a speech on television and felt that while everything they said made perfect sense, for some reason you couldn't buy what they were saying? Have you ever been talking to someone and got the distinct impression that they were speaking one way yet feeling another? If so you were probably dealing with a person who was working with a life lesson of Integrity.

As we are aware, we all have many different facets. Aligning each of these facets to send out a single congruent vibration is the challenge. The attribute of Integrity is defined as being able to align all these different facets and aspects to form one single harmonious, vibrational line of Integrity.

There are four lines of vibration within every person's energy field. These are the subtle vibrations that we transmit without conscious knowledge or thought. This is the 'energetic vibration' that precedes us before we walk into a room, or that allows friends at the other end of a telephone to 'pick up' on the fact that it is probably us who is calling. Mastering this life lesson depends on our ability to integrate these four lines.
These Four Vibrational Lines of Integrity comprise:

1. What we *speak*
2. How we *act*
3. What we *think*
4. What we *believe*

If one or more of these energetic lines do not match the others, the vibration we transmit will become blurred and unclear. At times, one line of vibration will cross over the others, canceling them out and blurring the overall signal that is transmitted into the universe. When that happens a blurred result is returned in all our creations, which in turn results in people having difficulty trusting or understanding us. In addition to being confusing, this also causes us to doubt ourselves, which of course, blurs our energy field even further.

A good example of this is the actor who is not totally convincing in a role. He may be perfectly competent, but for some reason we can't quite put our finger on, we just can't quite believe in the character enough to become fully engaged either with him or the play. In most cases, it's the fact that we know that something must be out of alignment for us to feel this way, but can't work out what it is, that prevents us from believing the performance. The actor is not being congruent. And try as they might to conceal it, the misalignment will be broadcast in their energy field. It is precisely this incongruency that often causes those uneasy feelings of mistrust when someone else is lying to us or being insincere.

Aligning our own personal lines of vibration is all that is required to place ourselves in a state of vibrational Integrity. When we are in vibrational Integrity, we interact well with others, which not only assists us in our dealings with them; it also makes it easier for us to fully connect and integrate with our higher self. Learning to walk consciously in total harmony is the most important step in the mastery of Integrity.

Interestingly enough, many people working with a life lesson of Integrity will actually choose a profession that puts them in the public eye. Some choose the stage, others choose politics, and some become sporting heroes.

Surprisingly enough, many even become spiritual leaders. They don't know they are not in integrity, of course. And because they don't see it, it's all too easy for us not to be overtly aware of it either. This is why it's so easy for people to be taken in by charlatans, false gurus, and other prominent leaders with ulterior motives. But by and large, most of us *do* pick it up on some level. It's as if our 'antennae' picks up on the fact that their energy field is being 'muddied' by a form of static.

Ironically, it is this very incoherence that is often responsible for making such people so attractive to us. We are not consciously aware of what it is about them that we find so fascinating. When we see something that's absolutely perfect, we barely give it a second thought as we pass by. Then we see something that is equally attractive, but has just one teeny tiny imperfection that causes it to be a fraction out of alignment, and we're mesmerized. We simply cannot take our eyes off of it, because we are transfixed by the incongruency in it. So it is with those people who, despite not being in integrity, still become movie stars or get elected to high office. In truth, people who are in integrity get nowhere near as much attention, because it is the flaws in a person's makeup that make them interesting.

Case History No. 15

Name: Max
Age: 57
Marital Status: Married
Profession: Congressman
Life Lesson: Integrity
Catalyst: Father
Type: Energy Stamp

Max is a businessman and a congressman. Many of the people who helped him build his organization are no longer with him. He has never learned how to keep people at a distance. He allows them in too close, and they begin to see his flaws, and they move on. Oddly enough, this has never hampered his ability to be successful. Even though he has been publicly attacked for some of the things he has done, and various people have tried to shame him and bring him down, Max simply sails past it all. He seems to have an almost uncanny talent for progression. Regardless of how badly he behaves, Max always manages to move onwards and upwards, because there are always more people willing to be suckered. Max is like a magician. You know it's all sleight of hand trickery, but you're so mesmerized by his adroitness that you simply can't wait to see what happens next. That's how people like Max go straight to the top.

Max's father was the unwitting catalyst for this life lesson. He had been a salesman all his life. Then one day, the light bulb went on and he realized that all the tricks of the trade he employed in his profession took him out of integrity, and the knowledge both appalled and paralyzed him. From that moment on, he was dead in the water. He became painfully aware when he was out of integrity, and his success faded as a result. Max saw his father's lack of success, and because of it, he found no merit in a man who was in integrity. Max wanted so badly to be a success, that he resolved that he would never be like his father.

So here we have two men, father and son, both working on the same life lesson of Integrity. One was making spectacular progress, seeing integrity issues in his life, which is the first sign of mastery, while the other resolutely refused to follow the same path. Over the years, plenty of people had tried to point out to Max where he was out of alignment, but he got real good at whitewashing, and he simply moved right on past it.

Max was about 57 when he first came to me. Apparently his daughter had a session with me, and had been so excited that she had told Max all about it. Out of curiosity he booked one too, just to see what I would tell him. He obviously didn't want to reveal much about himself. No doubt he wanted to test whether I was as good as his daughter thought I was.

As it happens, the Group never showed me what he did. They only showed me he was someone who both lived in the public eye and made decisions that affected a lot of people in similar circumstances. Once I revealed what I knew about him, I knew I had him. Now I was doing a bit of fortune telling.

As with all my private sessions, I try not to tell people what to do. Instead, I prefer to give them an overview of things, show them how their past histories have shaped their present, and what this means, so they can gain some understanding of their contracts and life lesson, and get a glimpse for themselves of what they are repeating and where this might be leading. If they can identify and acknowledge the patterns at work in their life, they can make the choice to change things or not.

It didn't take much for me to realize that, with Max, I barely had permission to talk about anything meaningful. He had called me out of curiosity, and even though I got the impression he was impressed with the accuracy of some of the things I was telling him, he really wasn't inclined to let that influence him enough to change anything he was doing. It was his choice. And since I am acutely aware that we should never try to take away anyone's power, I respected his right to choose his path for himself.

If Max had asked for my advice, that would have been different. I would have given him some suggestions, things he could do to help him master this life lesson, one of which is to ask people close to you for feedback on his behavior and actions. But since Max never invited it, it was not my place to force it upon him.

I never heard from Max again. I know he has retired from the public eye and is concentrating more on his business. As to whether he has ever made any attempt to heal this energy stamp, I cannot say. For some people, Max's father's about-turn might have been a positive catalyst. In Max's case, it turned out to be a negative one. That's how he set it up, of course, to give himself the opportunity to master this life lesson. As in all things, however, we have free choice. My guess is Max has chosen to ignore the set-ups he put in place, which would be a pity, since this means he will only have to come back and work on this same life lesson again.

Fig 6
Four vibrational lines of integrity in full integrity with each other send out a very clear signal that sets up the highest potential in all situations.

Fig 7

Four vibrational lines of integrity out of integrity with each other send out a very confused vibration that precedes the person in every interaction and everything they attempt to do.

Case History No. 16

Name: Caroline
Age: 64
Marital Status: Single
Profession: Film & TV Personality
Life Lesson: Integrity
Catalyst: Aunt
Type: Energy Matrix

Caroline was a real extrovert. Unfortunately, she was brought up by a straight-laced, fanatically religious aunt. The matriarch of the family, her aunt did everything she could to stifle Caroline's spontaneity. To Caroline's aunt, life was a serious business in which freedom was discouraged and one's responsibilities were to God, the church, and family in that order. Given Caroline's bubbly personality and independent spirit, it was a recipe for disaster. Caroline's aunt stuck rigidly to the old axiom that rules were meant to be obeyed, while Caroline was equally adamant that rules existed purely for the pleasure of breaking them. Not surprisingly, Caroline couldn't wait for the day when she could leave home.

With her extovert, larger than life personality, Caroline was well suited to a career in show business. The moment she graduated from school she packed a suitcase and headed for Hollywood. Although it took quite a while for her career to get started, once it did her disregard for convention and 'game for anything' attitude ensured her a regular place in the headlines. Over the years, she got a reputation for being a bit of a wild child whose wacky behavior and sometimes outrageous antics caused endless gossip and amusement. If a scandal erupted, you could be sure that Caroline's name would crop up somewhere. Of course, whatever Caroline did would be considered tame by today's standards, but for the time in which she lived, she was definitely considered one of the 'naughtier' girls of show biz. She never lied or tried to get out of trouble by covering things up or blaming other people. Rather, she would be happy to hold her hands up and, with a naughty grin, own up to whatever she had been caught doing. This worked to her benefit and really endeared her to the public. You just never knew was Caroline might be up to next, and that's what kept people riveted to her.

An accomplished comedy actress, Caroline was rarely off TV in the 70s and 80s, but once she started to wake up, she began to find her career less and less fulfilling. The industry was becoming less fun and more cutthroat, and she found herself having to work with people she described to me as "shallow and increasingly untalented." Once the studios started being run by accountants, and the emphasis shifted from providing high quality entertainment programs, to following whatever trend would produce the highest profits, she told me she could no longer tolerate the insincerity and lack of integrity that were becoming endemic. As she approached her 50th birthday, she made the brave decision to turn her back on show business and concentrate on her spiritual growth.

Like Max, Caroline booked a private session with me mostly out of curiosity. As soon as we started talking, I saw that there was very little I could actually tell her that she hadn't already worked out for herself. She had traveled a great deal in her quest for knowledge and enlightenment. She had read a lot of spiritual material, done a lot of inner work, and was pretty much set on her path to enlightenment. All in all, she was very content with her life. She had come to terms with a lot of things in her life, and had a fairly good understanding of who she was and what she had come here to do. She still had a lot of fans, and she used her 'old celebrity' status to good effect, drawing attention to various charities and personal causes.

The interesting thing about Caroline was that, without even knowing that she was working on a life lesson of Integrity, she had really grasped the essence of how to master it. Given that she had chosen not only to facilitate this through an energy matrix, and therefore, naturally had a blind spot about it, but also to spend most of her adult life in the notoriously fickle world of show business, she could easily have become a hypocrite - someone who was acutely attuned to insincerity and lack of integrity in others, but totally incapable of acknowledging it in herself.

To her credit, Caroline had paid a lot of attention to what went on around her, and had deduced that she wasn't always the best judge of her own behavior. She still had an extrovert personality, and she still enjoyed the limelight, so she knew how she might easily get sucked into situations where she might get pulled out of integrity and not be aware of it. Knowing her weak areas, however, she'd had the foresight to construct two safeguards. First, she did her best to avoid such situations. And secondly, she had schooled herself to pay close attention to others' reactions, and she used this feedback as a yardstick. She didn't get into trouble any more, but – and here's the best part – somehow she still managed to convey that naughty little 'will she-won't she?' twinkle that ensured people were never quite certain what she might do next. It's a very sexy trait and from what I could see, Caroline used it to very good effect.

As I said, there wasn't much I could do for Caroline, other than help her see how she was already mastering an important life lesson of Integrity and now it can be her strong point. She left the session with no great epiphanies with which to change her life, but she did have a new perspective which gave her a new view of her life and an inner confidence.

Primary Life Lesson #9

Love

Love of Self

The key to mastering the life lesson of Love lies in learning to Love our selves unconditionally and *first*. Love is the base energy of all that we call Universal Energy. All energy emanates from a foundation of Love, and we all experience this base energy as the *emotion* of Love. Emotions are the connecting link between the Energy Matrices and the Energy Tubes on which all life experiences are carried.

Living in a field of polarity, we humans need to experience one polarity in order to understand the opposite polarity. The strongest of all emotions is Love, and the opposite of (or polarity to) Love is Fear.

This is why those working with a primary life lesson of Love will often get stuck in a cycle of fear. Some draw the fear in through some form of drama. An example of this would be a person who gets wrapped up in conspiracy theories and dramas in general. Depending on where they are on their path to mastery, these people often appear to give love to everyone and everything. The problem is, in many instances, their motivation for doing so stems from their fear of being alone.

There are many aspects to this life lesson, the foremost of which involves developing the ability to love *oneself*. In order for people to see and experience love, they must be able to experience the direct opposite of love. The opposite of love is the vacuum that is left when no love is present. This vacuum is experienced as the emotion of fear. In the same way that *love* is the base of all energy,

so too is *fear* the base of all lack.
Fear is the origin of all negative emotions. But in the same way that darkness disappears when light shines upon it, so also can fear be overcome by the presence of love. Darkness is only a lack of light. Fear is only a lack of love.

The very first expression of Love, which is the most difficult for those learning to master this life lesson, is the love of *self*. To take this one step further, it is *only* possible to Love another to the degree that one loves one's self.

Throughout history, innumerable books have been written, songs have been sung, and wars have been fought in the name of, and supposedly for the Love of, God. Ironically, if we could only learn to direct our search for love inward, instead of outward, we would find that the oxymoronical phrase 'holy war' would quickly disappear from our vocabulary. God is within and not without. This is why we must learn to love *self* first. The expressions of love we will find in the new energy will be a direct reflection of this simple truth.

How many times have you heard people complaining of feeling unloved and lonely? They desperately want to find another person to share their life with, but love seems to keep eluding them. What they fail to understand is that the love they seek cannot be found when they are in a negative state. By telling themselves that they cannot be whole until another completes them, they are placing themselves in a vacuum. And what loving person would be attracted to a vacuum?

So many people say they are looking for love, when what they really mean is they are looking for someone to *love them*. They would have a lot more success if, instead of looking for a partner to love them, they concentrated on looking for ways to *give love*. For it is only through the act of *giving love* that we can set up the energy to *be love*, and therefore, to *receive love*.

In the higher vibrations of the new planet Earth we will start experiencing more unconditional Love. In the past, most of our relationships have been based on conditional love. Even our marriage vows are a statement of conditional love. This isn't to suggest that there is anything wrong with this. It is neither good nor bad. It is simply that the more unconditional love we incorporate into all our relationships, the easier it will be for these relationships to evolve into higher dimensions.

Case History No. 17

Name: Sam
Age: 40
Marital Status: Single
Profession: Business Manager
Life Lesson: Love
Catalyst: Mother
Type: Energy Matrix

As mentioned in The Seven Stages of Life, most of us choose an energy role model outside our immediate family. In Sam's case, however, he chose to model himself upon his mother. On the face of it, that might not seem like a bad thing. Sam's mother was a lovely lady whose greatest goal in life had always been to have a successful marriage with a loving husband and a family. As far as she was concerned, this was the greatest accomplishment a person could aspire to. And to her credit, she succeeded in creating precisely what she wanted.

Sam's male and female sides were so well balanced, he had no problem speaking from the heart and openly expressing his feelings. As a result he had no problem attracting women. Sam was looking for love. Not just any love, but the same great love that his mother had for and with his father. But for some reason, the *grande passion* he was so desperately seeking seemed to keep eluding him. The result was, Sam found himself bouncing from one relationship to another. This began to bother him, as he didn't regard himself as a playboy, and certainly didn't relish the idea of gaining a reputation as such. All he was trying to do was recreate the same thing his mother had been so successful at creating.

What Sam didn't know, however, was that his mother had never actually loved her husband. She had merely created a situation and a set of circumstances that cleverly gave her the illusion that she had succeeded in what she'd set out to do. She had never been in love; she had simply settled for someone who appeared to be going in the same direction as she was.

When Sam first called for a consultation, the one thing that kept coming up was relationships. By his own admission, he had enjoyed some beautiful relationships with some wonderful women, and when they'd ended he had always managed to stay friends with his ex-lovers. There was never any bad feeling. When he left someone, he left the relationship as a friend. The truth was, Sam was really only ever friends with them to begin with. This often happens with people who are looking for love. They desperatley want everyone to think well of them, so when their relationships end they work to ensure that everyone involved still thinks well of them. This also is very common with people working with the life lesson of love.

The biggest challenge - and Sam's biggest blind spot - was that he did not love himself. He spent all his time and energy falling in and out of relationships, looking for the 'right' person to fall in love and settle down with, and trying to create a meaningful relationship with each of the women he got involved with, but none of his partners ever really got to know who he is because he does not love himself. In essence, Sam was actually looking for a woman who could love him enough to make him whole.

Since it was very evident to me that relationships were Sam's biggest challenge, I started out by saying to him, "Relationships seem to be an area that is a big enigma to you." To which he replied, "No. I have lots of them."

"Ah, but is that what you want?" I asked.

"No." He replied. "I'd really like to settle down, but I haven't seemed to have met the right woman; someone with whom I can be happy on a consistent basis."

Without realizing it, Sam was revealing that the reason all his relationships failed was because he was looking outside himself for the love and acceptance that could only come from within.

I then started to draw Sam out about his parents' relationship with one another. I asked a few pointed questions designed to cause him to take another look at his mother's attitude toward his father. In so doing, he not only began to re-assess his perception of the idyllic relationship he had always believed they'd had; he also began to realize that, though she had never consciously set out to do so, his mother had been the negative catalyst for him in this situation. Once Sam saw that the role model he had been patterning himself after all this time was not going to fit for him, he was more open to exploring the situation a little deeper.

"So, how do you feel about yourself?" I then asked him.

"I feel empty inside," he admitted. "The times I feel best are when I am in love with someone and can make them happy. When it happens, I just shine, because I know I am

really good at it."
Did that make him happy? I inquired.

It did in the beginning, Sam confessed. But it never lasted
long. Once the feelings started to fade, things would
peter out and he and his girlfriend would end up parting as
friends.

"And then what happens?" I asked.

"Then I find someone else and fall in love all over again.
You know," Sam said, as realization suddenly began to
dawn, "I seem to fall in love a lot."

"First of all," I said to Sam, "Understand that if you're happy
with that, then it's okay. There's nothing wrong with it. But
if you're not happy with it then you need to look at how
you are feeling on an inner level. If you feel empty inside,
ask yourself: Would *you* like to fall in love with someone
who feels empty inside? Would *you* like to be the piece
that completes someone else? Are you looking for two
half people to come together in the hope that they will
make one whole person? Because if you are, it isn't going
to work well, because when that happens, if one person
should move the other invariably falls.

That first session with Sam continued in a similar vein, with
me asking questions in such a way that he could not help
but begin to identify some of the patterns in his life, and
particularly his love life. The last time we spoke, it was
evident that Sam was beginning to change. He had a new
relationship, and though I didn't think this one was going
to last either, it was obvious that, now that he understood
his process, Sam was making a concerted effort to do
things differently. As a result, he was no longer relying on
someone else to make him feel complete. That, in itself, is
a big step in the right direction towards self-love.

One of the most important things we need to know about relationships in the higher dimensions is that the more we learn to practice unconditional love, the fewer unrealistic expectations we will have of our partners, thus the less opportunity there is for us to be disappointed, or for things to go wrong.

On the other side of the fence, Fiona's story, below, provides us with a perfect example of what can happen when a person working on this life lesson gets stuck in a cycle of drama and fear.

Case History No. 18

Name: Fiona
Age: 49
Marital Status: Divorced
Profession: Accountant
Life Lesson: Love
Catalyst: Mother (not covered in story)
Type: Energy Stamp

Fiona was a drama queen. She grew up in a household that revolved around her and her moods. She was always creating some sort of incident or drama in her life to make her the center of attention. And she was very good at it. There is no judgment about that. We all love our little dramas. It's why we go to see plays and the movies. Drama adds excitement to our lives.

As Fiona grew, her love of drama and excitement started becoming more of a problem. Fiona became a magnet for trouble. By the time she was a teenager, her parents were pulling their hair out, wondering what she would get up to next. It seemed like a disaster when she got pregnant while she was still at school. But marriage and motherhood seemed to settle her down. Having a family gave Fiona a different focus for a while. There's enough natural drama that goes on in a family to satisfy most people's need or urge for drama and excitement.

After Fiona's children were grown, she divorced her first husband and then remarried within just a few months. That's when she started being attracted to 'light work." At least, that's what she told me, before she launched into a long and enthusiastic conversation peppered with excited references to 'secret governments," "the illuminati," "reptilians'" and other non-humans aliens having control over us, etc. It was not long before I became aware that our session was no longer a two-sided conversation. Instead, it had become an oppertunity for her to tell me all about the beings that had control over her is some way. Fiona was entirely engulfed in her fear-based dramas.

It was hard to believe that a 49-year-old woman with adult children and a responsible career as a CPA could get so excited about such fear-based subjects. When I was finally able to get a word in edge-wise, it only took a few questions for me to understand Fiona's situation.

Fiona had never found any fulfillment in any of her close relationships. Consequently, she'd chosen to fill the hole created by the lack of love in her life, with the opposite emotion of fear. She wasn't interested in hearing about life lessons. She'd called me for one reason and one reason only: to feed her need for drama and excitement by contriving to get from me some evidence that she could then use as fodder in her next "conspiracy theory" conversation.

Since we all have free will to choose our path in life, there was nothing else I could do other than to wish Fiona well, and leave our conversation at that.

Primary Life Lesson #10

Trust

Trusting Self

The life lesson of Trust is a simple lesson to understand, but a very difficult one to master.

If the those experiencing this life lesson choose a positive catalyst to help facilitate this lesson, it will generally be in the form of a mother or father who encourages them to believe that they can do anything they want to, if they only put their mind to it.

If people set up a contract for a negative catalyst, however, it will often appear in the form of a parent that abuses them, thereby ensuring that they quickly learn to not trust anyone, least of all themselves. In this instance, the life lesson would be facilitated as an energy stamp. Ultimately the life lesson of Trust is about learning to trust one's own self above all others.

When we lived in the lower (First Wave) vibrational energy, we believed in the concept of "follow the leader." But all that is changing. Now that we are moving toward a higher vibrational level, there's a new 'Second Wave' concept that dictates, 'follow one's self.'

People working with a primary life lesson of Trust will often have a very difficult time learning to trust themselves, and with learning to accept and hold their own power.

Once this life lesson is mastered, however, they often appear to walk through life with an inner sense of direction, always looking and acting as if they know exactly where they are going. In actuality, they will finally have learned to trust themselves enough to *no longer need to know.*

The interesting thing about Trust is that few of us have a problem placing our trust in God. But virtually all of us have a big problem accepting that we *are* God.

Trust is an extremely important life lesson to master, for Trust allows us to become part of the whole by placing us in the flow of Universal Energy. When we lack trust, we lack faith.

Once we learn to Trust, we can allow ourselves to be vulnerable. When we allow ourselves to be vulnerable we turn our weaknesses into strengths. In fact, as we are going to learn from the Crystal Children that are now being born, our vulnerability *is* the source of our greatest strength.

Case History No. 19

Name: Joanna
Age: 35
Marital Status: Divorced
Profession: Healer, Internet Entrepreneur
Life Lesson: Trust
Catalyst: Mother
Type: Energy Stamp

From a very young age, Joanna was forced to suffer repeated sexual abuse at the hands of her father. Obviously, that's a very tough thing for any child to have to deal with. What was even worse, however, was that in Joanna's case, her mother colluded with it. She knew it

212 - Spiritual Psychology

was happening, and intentionally looked the other way. So, as often happens with people working on this life lesson, right from the outset, Joanna was forced to deal with issues of trust. After all, if your own parents betray your trust, who else is left? Having grown up with having her trust betrayed over and over again, Joanna's life unfolded with repeated experience of the self-fulfilling prophecy that people are not to be trusted. Time and time again she attracted people into her life who proved her right. Virtually every boyfriend she ever had let her down. A friend with whom she had set up a healing practice embezzled money from their business account. When she thought she had finally found a man who was trustworthy, she immediately married him, only to find out later that he was an inveterate womanizer. To date, Joanna's husband has had at least four affairs that she is aware of. Like her mother before her, Joanna feigned ignorance of her husband's betrayal. She couldn't bring herself to confront him, any more than she could bring herself to confront her mother about turning a blind eye while Joanna's father abused her.

After years of being miserable, of knowing that something big was missing from her life, Joanna embarked on a spiritual quest. She started going to seminars, attending workshops, reading books, anything that could give her some insight into the patterns of her life and connect her with the missing parts of herself. Eventually, she stumbled across our work, and after reading our books, decided to attend one of our seminars.

Joanna's secondary life lesson was Definition, and as it happened, the more she worked on herself, the more she began to learn how to define herself and draw firm boundaries. Once she started to define herself, she slowly began to start trusting herself. About a year after we first met, Joanna did something she never would have considered doing before. She decided to start a business

all by herself, selling flower remedies on the Internet.
She took it slowly, starting out small, so that the business
wouldn't interfere with her day job.

Then something wonderful happened. The hospital she
had been working at for years asked Joanna to manage
and oversee an experimental program, involving trials
with complementary therapies and integrative healing
modalities. Joanna was in seventh heaven. It dovetailed
perfectly with all the things she had always been interested
in. She still kept her Internet business going, and as it too
began to become more profitable, the more her confidence
in herself grew. With two successes in her life, Joanna
began to blossom. Her relationship with her husband still
wasn't perfect, but it too started showing signs of change
as her husband's respect for her increased.

The last time I spoke to Joanna, she told me that she had
got in touch with her father and confronted him with what
he had done. To her surprise, he took full responsibility for
his actions and apologized for all the hurt he had caused.
Sadly, she never did resolve things with her mother, who
died a very bitter woman. Ironically, all the guilt Joanna's
mother felt had turned inward into self-hatred and anger.
But unlike Joanna's dad, her mom had not been able
to take responsibility for her actions, and instead she
projected all her own self-anger at Joanna.

Joanna is a good example of someone who, having
started out with most of the cards stacked against her,
has had the courage and fortitude to accept where she
was and take charge of her life and change the energy
stamp. Responsibility is the balance of power. As I have
said previously: To increase personal power, find ways
of increasing personal responsibility. Here Joanne took
responsibility for her own life and increased her own
powers of creation.

Case History No. 20

Name: Meryl
Age: 40
Martial Status: Divorced
Profession: Psychotherapist
Life Lesson: Trust
Catalyst: Father
Type: Energy Matrix

In my first telephone session with Meryl, we identified her life lesson as Trust. I also identified a contract that was about to be activated with a little girl. Since she is divorced and not currently in a relationship, this caught Meryl off guard. She didn't know if she should be scared, or if I was totally crazy. As the conversation progressed I discovered that this child was about to enter her life in order to activate a back-up plan. Once Meryl was able to breathe again, I was able to show her that this was the same little girl she had miscarried in between her two sons. Meryl then told me that one of her sons was about to become a father and that she would watch for this child with great interest.

Just prior to publication of this book Meryl attended one of our week-long OverLight Spiritual Psychology trainings. Unfortunately, when she showed up we did not appear to have her registered, even though she had signed up online. We assumed that this was simply a technical error.

In the OverLight trainings we not only teach the material in this book, we also work on each other as part of the training process. Each participant gets to do several sessions using their own methods, while attempting to incorporate the material we teach in our course. I do several short demonstration sessions on stage to show people how this material can be applied. Despite the fact that this requires laying out one's entire life in front of others, there is usually a long waiting list of volunteers. Many of the people attending the OverLight trainings are professional psychologists, psychiatrists, medical doctors or psychotherapists and I have found them surprisingly eager to work on themselves in public. These demonstration sessions are staged with two chairs facing one another. The chair the client occupies is affectionately called the "hot seat."

My estimate is that sixty to eighty percent of all women on earth have been sexually abused in some way. As it transpired, when it came to Meryl's turn to occupy the hot seat it soon became apparent that she was one of these brave souls. I told the class that Meryl had obviously been imprinted with an energy stamp from her father that had given her the perfect opportunity to work with her life lesson of Trust. Meryl bravely allowed us to lay bare her life in front of the others in the class, as we went on to identify her secondary life lesson as Definition and then showed her how her own blind spots in both areas had affected the course of her life. The interesting part is that Meryl was very close to mastering her secondary life lesson, but was still very vulnerable when it came to trusting. She revealed that she always felt as though she was invisible. As she left the hot seat everyone was deeply touched by her tremendous courage. Although she didn't realize it at the time, the fact that she had allowed herself to be so vulnerable was a big step toward mastering her life lesson of Trust. However it was not until later that week that I discovered what was really going on.

On the final day of training, emotions were naturally running very high. That was when an interesting event occurred with Meryl that clearly illustrated for me the difference between a Trust lesson that is facilitated by an energy stamp versus a Trust lesson that is facilitated by an energy matrix.

Barbara was passing out receipts to the participants when she came to Meryl. For some reason Meryl's receipt was missing. Barbara apologized and said that she would go up to our room and print out a new one. Despite having gone a long way towards mastering this life lesson, this simple little incident triggered enormous issues within Meryl, in which all of her previous feeling of abandonment and invisibility resurfaced. She excused herself and fled to the bathroom where we later discovered she had broken down in tears.

The point to note here is that I was wrong about Meryl. This incident demonstrated that she was not working with an energy stamp after all; she was working with an energy matrix. Although her father had indeed played the role of negative catalyst which led me to think we were working with an energy stamp. The reality was that Meryl was always going to unconsciously attract such experiences because she was wired this way.

To illustrate this, when Barbara immediately went to our room to print out Meryl's receipt, she discovered that the original had been in her hand all the time. Initially, she was very upset, believing that through her own inefficiency she had unwittingly caused a great deal of misery for Meryl. But as I explained to everybody later, Meryl herself had unconsciously created this situation through her own energetic wiring.

Meryl couldn't understand why, if she was so close to mastery, how come she had such a strong reaction to such a small incident. Once I explained to her and the class that this was an energy matrix that would be with her throughout her life, and that she will always have a tendency to draw people and events into her life that are designed to trigger her trust issues, Meryl has the choice to take a higher view when such events occur. This is the art of mastery.

> **Case History No. 21**
> Name: Cathy
> Age: 56
> Marital Status: Divorced
> Profession: Publisher
> Life Lesson: Trust
> Catalyst: Mother
> Type: Energy Stamp

Like our previous case study, Joanne, Cathy also had the rug pulled out from under her at the outset. The difference in Cathy's case, however, is that the process started to happen even *before* she was born. Cathy's father died at a very young age, leaving her mother with five young boys to care for and Cathy on the way.

Cathy grew up in a poor family, in a poor community. By the time she was two, her mother was so worn out from trying to keep a roof over her family's head and food in their stomachs, she became sick and unable to look after them. Cathy and her older brothers were sent to live in an orphanage while their mother recovered.

Throughout the ten years she lived in the orphanage, Cathy felt like an observer, someone who was constantly having to stay alert, to keep her eyes open, and watch and listen for that 'unexpected curve' that might get thrown at her. Young as she was, Cathy had deduced that the world was an unsafe place. She couldn't rely on people to behave the way they ought to behave, so she had better never let down her guard.

Cathy's mother loved her kids, but having grown up in an undemonstrative family herself, she'd never learned how to express affection. Displays of affection embarrassed her. She never hugged or kissed her kids. Because she didn't know how to respond when they tried to hug her, she would brush them off with a curt "Don't be silly," or simply turn her back and walk away. To Cathy, it looked like rejection. Consequently, she grew up feeling unloved, unwanted and unable to rely on anyone but herself. All her brothers were very talented and intelligent young men. Two of them won scholarships to college, as did Cathy herself. But while Cathy's mom scrimped and scraped to help her boys get a college education, she refused to let Cathy do the same. She said she needed Cathy to earn a paycheck so she could help out at home. What I saw was that as her only daughter and her last child, Cathy's mom couldn't bear to let Cathy out of her sight. But Cathy didn't know that at the time. She just assumed that her mom loved her brothers much more than she loved her.

Cathy met her first husband when she was seventeen. She didn't trust him any more than she had trusted anyone else in her life, but she was desperate for love, and any excuse to get away from home. By the time she was 21 she was married with two young children. Five years later, her husband ran off with another woman. In time she met another man. But that relationship ended abruptly the moment she discovered he already had a wife. After spending several more years on her own, she had a third relationship with a man who seemed to be very serious, responsible and steady. Still, she'd become so paranoid about betrayal that it took her another four years to decide whether she should marry him.

As it transpired, Cathy had only been married a month when she discovered that her second husband had a secret. He was hooked on gambling. Cathy went into shock. She couldn't believe that she had picked the wrong man again!

From a higher perspective, of course, every single one of

Cathy's relationship had been perfectly set up to help her confront and overcome her issues with the life lesson of Trust. But, of course, she was not aware of it. The only thing she could see was that, either there was something about *her* that seemed to attract the worst kind of men, or she was a lousy judge of character.

Feeling that she had more than enough evidence to justify her belief that she couldn't trust anyone, Cathy swore that she would never again make the mistake of putting her emotions or her financial security into the hands of someone else. She became very cynical and aloof where men were concerned. For the next several years, her life consisted of her children, her career and her relatives. That was it. She saw her mom regularly, but it was more out of a sense of duty than anything else. Their relationship was so prickly, that neither could say the time they spent together was cozy, or even particularly pleasant.

The big turning point in Cathy's life came in her early 40s when she went along with a friend to see a regression therapist. What happened during her session proved to be so profound that, even though Cathy put it all down to her imagination, something inside her underwent a fundamental shift. The way she described it to me was that, for the first time in her entire life, she felt herself "relaxing and settling into herself." Suddenly, she felt like someone had removed the glass window through which she had been observing life. She no longer felt she had to be a detached observer, constantly on her guard. Though she still couldn't grasp everything on a conscious level, she began to sense there was a reason she'd gone through all her experiences.

Soon after, Cathy met a man who was several years younger than her. Suddenly, she found herself doing the unthinkable: she actually surrendered to the situation and embarked on a passionate a relationship with him. For once, Cathy didn't concern herself with whether or not she could trust someone, whether they would lie to her, betray her, or cheat on her. Sure, she was a little concerned about what people might think about the age gap, but she put that aside and went ahead anyway.

It was the best and most healing thing Cathy could have done for herself. Finally, by allowing herself to surrender and simply accept the love she was being given, as well as the love she felt, Cathy did the best thing she could possibly do for herself. The difference it made to her life was profound. Having finally let down her barriers, even her relationship with her mother began to change.

Cathy and her lover were together for five years. It was the most healing, joyous, unconditionally loving relationship she had ever experienced. The most interesting thing about this relationship was that neither of them left the other. There was no betrayal, no rejection and no loss of love. They simply "knew" when the time had come for their relationship to move to a different level. To this day, they are still the very best of friends. In learning to put aside her fears and to trust herself and her instincts, Cathy had healed her energy stamp. And in doing so, she let go all of the resentment and repressed anger that had prevented her from understanding and accepting her mother. She was able to make her peace with her mother just before her mother died.

Primary Life Lesson #11

Truth

Responsibility

As we proceed from one life lesson to another, it is important to remember that each life lesson can look quite different depending on the level of mastery an individual has attained. Truth provides us with a vivid example of these differences.

The life lessons of Truth and Trust are very close to each other and thus are often confused. When a person chooses to master Truth, their energetic wiring is such that they will have difficulty discerning and standing in their own Truth. Since this can appear, at first glance, as if they do not trust themselves, I ask more questions than usual in order to determine the larger picture of overall patterns before deciding which of these two similar life lessons they are working with. Sometimes, I even use the simple direct technique of asking: "If I asked you to describe the main focus of your life as being one of Trust or Truth, which would it be?"

When one has difficulty standing in their own truth, they will always have a tendency to adopt the truth of others in place of their own. They will always be looking for the newest book, or the latest concept, idea or system to follow.

Truth ~ A Blind Spot

When a person is at an early stage of mastery, they usually are incapable of being truly honest with themselves This is a very difficult place for any one to be at, since we never really know where we are, and, therefore, we will always feel compelled to measure ourselves against others. Not only is truth elusive to us, but we will often create illusions to rationalize our choices.

At this stage of mastery, those who choose to facilitate this life lesson as an energy matrix will seek any way possible to avoid taking responsibility for their actions. They often get caught in a loop, looking outside themselves for guidelines, rather than discerning their own. Sometimes this will create a problem with honesty towards others. They may tell lies and create excuses, rather than be honest about what is really going on in their life. In many cases they may live in a fantasy world. The big challenge comes when they really start believing their own lies, as this creates a full disconnection from themselves.

When one is working with Truth at a higher level of mastery it is quite common to become a teacher or a leader who is capable of encompassing many varied flavors of truth without attachment to any one flavor in particular. Mastery of this life lesson also leads to the understanding that truth is based entirely on one's own perception and that it is through the art of shifting perception that one can see many truths beyond one's own.

Brutal Honesty

Mastery of this attribute can only be accomplished through brutal honesty with one's self. This means taking full responsibility for one's own thoughts and actions. It does not mean that those thoughts or actions need to be perfect. . . they need only to be *one's own*. Once you start taking responsibility for your own reality, your mastery of Truth will begin. These people will be permanent seekers, always looking for answers to their questions. They will deny their own impressions, feelings and thoughts and take on others' instead.

Through the Eyes of Others

Those new to this life lesson usually see themselves entirely through the eyes of other people. They can clearly see from the perspective of others, but they have a blind spot when it comes to their own truth. These are the people who always judge themselves by what *they* think others are thinking of *them*.

Truth is a very difficult attribute to master. So, rather than judging those who are working on this life lesson, we should love them unconditionally and applaud their courage, because the challenges are very great. Even if it takes several lifetimes, mastering this life lesson has the effect of moving the whole of humanity forward.

Case History No. 22

Name: Keith
Age: 52
Marital Status: Married
Profession: CEO of a multinational company
Life Lesson: Truth
Catalyst: Father
Type: Energy Matrix

Keith is a very powerful man. For years, others who seek the truth have been drawn to him because they see him as someone who has a definite handle on what is truly important in life, and what isn't. And for the most part, their faith in Keith is justified. He is a wonderful counselor, visionary and advisor. Ironically, however, Keith has enormous difficulties standing in his own Truth.

Keith has been married for many years to a woman with whom he no longer has anything in common. For more than twelve years, he has slept alone in the spare room. Keith's marriage is devoid of all emotion and affection. The only thing keeping them together is their son.

Truth is Keith's blind spot. Even when he is telling people what he sees, he does it in such a way that he almost negates himself. Instead of coming right out and saying what he means, he dissembles and beats around the bush. Rather than disagree with someone, he will say, "Well, I understand your point of view, but, you know, someone taught me such and such, so maybe you might want to consider looking at it from that perspective." Because he has such a problem with recognizing the truth, he finds it very difficult to have the courage of his own convictions. So he spends his life, bouncing from one truth to another, accepting whatever appears to be the prevailing opinion.

Growing up, Keith developed a belief system which dictated that success is a good job with a six-figure income, a comfortable roomy house in the suburbs with one wife, 2.4 children and a two-car garage. To leave all that behind simply because he does not have any love, affection or communication with his wife would mark him out as a huge failure, or so Keith believes. So, instead, he puts up with being unloved, unfulfilled and unhappy. On the few occasions he has had the opportunity to experience love on an equal footing with another woman, he has always pulled back the moment she started asking for a commitment.

Keith genuinely believes that the greatest gift he can give his son is a stable, happy home life with two parents that love him. The truth is, Keith is doing his son a huge disservice by teaching him that it is "normal" for a man to be out of integrity and to live a lie.

Keith's lesson, if he would but see it, is not to preserve the status quo, at the expense of his own integrity and happiness, but rather, to have the courage of his convictions, to find out what is really important to him (as opposed to accepting others' truths and standards), and live a life that is in alignment with his soul purpose.

Sadly, Keith cannot bring himself to do anything that would upset the status quo. This wonderful loving man is totally stuck. Despite all his good intentions, if he cannot learn to work with Truth and walk in his own Truth, he simply won't be able to complete this life lesson.

Case History No. 23

Name: Leslie
Age: 42
Marital Status: Divorced
Profession: Owns PR Firm
Life Lesson: Truth
Catalyst: Father
Type: Energy Stamp

Leslie was the youngest of five children, and a real 'Daddy's girl.' Dad was working with a life lesson of Integrity. He was a real smooth talker and a brilliant salesman. He could look you straight in the eye and tell you black was white and you would believe him. He was such a charmer, and so convincing that even when people knew he was lying they couldn't bring themselves to contradict him. Leslie so adored and admired her Daddy that she was only too happy to act as though she believed his lies.

Worse yet, Leslie even came to believe that it was acceptable to act out of integrity. In fact, she even chose a career that gave her every opportunity to follow in Daddy's footsteps. She carved out a very successful career in public relations, and pretty soon, just like Daddy, Leslie began to believe her own lies.

Things went well for a time. Leslie started her own public relations company and became very successful. But the more she acted out of integrity, the more unbalanced her life became, and the more things started to unravel. She started having problems with her staff. They became unreliable. They were lazy. They started betraying her by switching to rival agencies and taking their clients with them. Leslie was furious. *How could they do this to me?* She raged. *Didn't they have any sense of loyalty?* Because she had a big blind spot about Truth, it never once occurred to Leslie that the people around her were merely mirroring back to her what she herself had been sending out.

When Leslie first called me, I commenced our conversation in the usual way, outlining what she could expect from the session. I always set the tone for the conversation so that clients do not surrender their power to me in any way and also so that they are not surprised if I should refuse to take their power from them in the event they try to give it to me. What I usually tell them is: "This work is about empowerment and, therefore, I am *not* going to tell you which way to turn, nor am I going to tell you what you should or should not do. The whole point of these sessions is to simply show you your own life patterns from a different perspective so that you can see all of your choices more clearly."

With Leslie, however, I could not even get these two sentences out before she started telling me that she does sessions all the time with many different healers, readers and psychics and there was no need to tell her any of this. She obviously thought that the fact that she had seen so many people was sufficient to give her some advantage in our session. I was not impressed and I told her that I had *not* done sessions with any other intuitive healer, and thus I always insisted on telling every client what to expect from a session with me.

As soon as we began, Leslie started trying to take control of the conversation by asking me to verify all the information she had received in her last reading. It quickly became apparent that she was not in fact calling me for a consultation, but rather, simply wanted me to validate what she had already heard from other people. Leslie had become wrapped up in a story she'd been told about a past life which was responsible for all the difficulties she was presently experiencing. I quickly saw that Leslie was caught in this loop and if I played along with it I would only be enabling her to remain stuck. She was completely caught off guard when I told her that I thought she was working with a life lesson of Truth and asked her about her current relationship with her father. She immediately started stumbling, asking what this had to do with the failure of her business. When I explained that I believed that her father had played the important role of catalyst for her life lesson of Truth, which was one of the primary reasons for her current business challenges, Leslie was so stunned, she let me proceed.

It's important to point out here that I generally do not jump right into identifying primary life lessons in my private sessions, and that I only do this when I feel it would be helpful for a client to see the larger picture. But in Leslie's case, I knew that my time was limited. Even though she had paid for a forty-five minute session, I was aware of the need to grab her attention right up front, or I would never get the chance to reach her. So, trusting my own intuition, I closed my eyes and began to describe Leslie's father as if I had known him all my life.

From that moment on, I knew I had Leslie's undivided attention. I asked her what had happened six years before that had caused a big shift in her relationship with her father that still remained unresolved. Stunned that I had been so accurate, even to the point of giving her the date, Leslie admitted that this was when she'd had a big showdown with her father. For the first time in her life, Leslie had confronted her dad with one of his own lies. He became very angry and they have not spoken since. Leslie felt immense guilt about this and still doubted if she had done the right thing. She even told me that she knew she shouldn't have done it, and that she would rather have lived with his lies than confront him with the truth.

I congratulated Leslie for standing in her own truth and then began telling her about the Twelve Primary Life Lessons and the attributes of a person working with a life lesson of Truth. I even suggested that she forget about her Dad right now and focus on getting clear about what was in her own heart. I told her that as the president of this corporation she was responsible for setting the overall tone of her company and that her constant search for truth outside of herself was confusing everyone around her. Her response to this was: "But what if I'm wrong?" Then all she needed to do, I reminded her, was to simply change her perspective on what constituted truth for her. The important thing to know about truth is that it is not a stationery object, but rather an evolutionary process. As we grow and evolve so too does our perception of 'truth.'

At the end of the session Leslie begged me either to extend the time or allow her to call again the following day. Fortunately for Leslie neither option was possible. Leslie had to wait five months for the next session.

When we next spoke, Leslie was excited. Her business was starting to turn around with what felt like very little effort from her. In fact, she even wondered whether the changes that were taking place had anything to do with her new perceptions at all. She was also very excited to tell me about what had happened with her father. She had received a call from him one day, just as if nothing had happened. He'd even called her by the pet name that he had used when she was growing up. Fortunately, Leslie now understood that it was not her place to change her father. The only thing she was responsible for was standing in her own truth. While this was wonderful for me to hear, it was important for me to apply the acid test. When I asked Leslie how many readings she'd had since we had last spoken, she proudly reported that she had not had any, as she had finally started listening to her own inner guidance, and following what was in her heart.

At the end of this session Leslie briefly slipped and once again asked if I would consider doing a session with her every week. I gently explained to her that I had already given her most of what she needed, and that it was against my policy to do this too frequently. There are people who do great work with others as mentors. Yet, due to my own schedule being booked so far in advance, this was simply not a possibility for me to offer. I reassured her that the more she learned to trust her own inner guidance, the less she would need to seek any answers outside of herself. The key to finding one's answers in a life lesson of Truth, I told her, lay, not in the search, but rather, in the formulation of the questions. One only has to formulate the question to find that the answer comes from within. All she needed to do at that point was to accept the answer as truth for her... in that moment.

I still do sessions with Leslie about once a year, and I have come to really look forward to them. As is true with most people reaching the upper levels of mastery in a life lesson of Truth, Leslie has become a person that others now come to for direction. She is known as a "librarian of truth,"

Primary Life Lesson #12

Grace

Walking in Harmony with All Things

Grace is the final step to Mastery. In addition to being the very last life lesson we work to master, Grace is also the most beautiful. In this life lesson, a person learns that it really is not the destination that is important. What really matters is the journey itself, as well as the grace with which we experience the journey.

To understand the importance of this life lesson it may help to ask yourself this question: How often do I awaken in the morning and say, "I love my life, I can't wait to see what today holds"?

This may sound like a simple exercise in positive thinking, but in reality it is much more. When you truly see yourself as a player of the game, and allow yourself to play the game with Grace, then the mastery of all the remaining energy matrices becomes not only much easier but also much more enjoyable.

Do you find that you long for Home? Do you feel like you woke up one day in that uncomfortable body you inhabit and spend the majority of your energy trying to find your way back Home? If the answer to these questions is yes, then you have not yet mastered the life lesson of Grace. Few people have, as not many people get to work on this life lesson.

Grace is the one life lesson that very few people choose or get to work with. In fact, I have met only one person that I know to be working with a life lesson of Grace. That is the reason you will only see one case history under this section. What's really important to understand about this life lesson is that most people believe that once we have mastered this final lesson, we become so "perfect" we can almost walk on water. We don't. We still have our challenges, as do people working with a life lesson of Grace.

Grace is the connection to what the Group calls the Universal Energy. This is the energy that connects all things. A life lesson of Grace strengthens your connection to the energy that runs between and connects all things. In human form, we naturally have the illusion that we are separate from one another. Although this is not yet proven scientific fact, it is widely understood that there is a connection between everything that exists. The connection to the Universal Energy is often experienced as your connection to your higher self or your spiritual connection.

At first glance it's easy to confuse Grace with the life lesson of Charity (which is walking in harmony with other people). When one walks in mastery of this life lesson they intuitively know and work in harmony with all things on all levels. Many of the stories of master teachers throughout our history are accurately describing a person who is stepping into mastery of this exact life lesson. This connection will allow an understanding of time, space and energy that very few have ever experienced up to this point in the history of mankind.

Due to the nature of the Grace attributes, it is always the final life lesson to be mastered. In fact, since most souls are complete with the Earth experience after they master eight to ten life lessons, very few people ever work with the life lesson of Grace. This draws a picture of a very sacred contract only taken by the elite of souls. Believe me when I say that the brave souls who do work with a life lesson of

Grace rarely feel like they are special. Instead, they feel like they have a handicap that no one else has.

One working with Grace as a primary life lesson always looks for the largest picture possible since they are looking for how everything is connected. They aren't the slightest bit interested in the secrets of life, they want to know the secrets of the Universe. They will deal with people perfectly well but will also see the interdimensional parts of each one of us and internally know truth when they hear, see or experience it in any form.

In teaching the Spiritual Psychology courses, when I speak about Grace, it is everyone's first choice in identifying their own life lesson. Please keep in mind here what I said earlier, that you will see yourself in every life lesson and because you have a built-in blind spot in order to facilitate your life lesson, it is most difficult to identify your own. In Grace everyone can see a little of themselves yet it is extremely rare that a person is ever working with a life lesson of Grace.

Case History No. 24

Name: Nancy
Age: 72 and growing younger every day.
Marital Status: Widow
Profession: Author, Healer, Teacher
Life Lesson: Grace with secondary of Acceptance
Catalyst: Father
Type: Energy Matrix

Nancy is a very beautiful, very old soul. Barbara and I met her when she hosted one of our seminars. It was immediately obvious to me that Nancy was a teacher, but, of course, she herself has no patience with that description. As with many things in Nancy's life, this description simply does not cover enough. She still has all the same problems as everyone else. She still feels that there is so much yet to accomplish. And she still wonders what she is doing here on Earth. Her greatest desire is to feel that she has connected on every level to every thing.

Nancy has an inner knowing and has learned to trust her own guidance. The inner knowing has given her the ability to extract only the very essence from everything that passes her way. When she reads a book she intuitively skips over the passages that are meaningless or incorrect to her and takes only the parts that validate a truth she has garnered deep within. Even with this inner direction, however, she is still confused as to why life on Earth is not a lot easier and more fulfilling. Above all, Nancy knows how to laugh and that perspective gets her through any situation she may find herself in. She calls herself a gatherer. In reality she is a teacher who attracts other people who are searching for the larger answers.

Nancy's husband died just a few weeks before our first meeting. She saw this as a huge completion in her life. She understood that she had done her duty by him with love and understanding and that she was now free to begin a new phase of her life with a larger focus. Attempting to put words and a definition to that focus was now the most challenging part of Nancy's life. What she didn't realize was that, all along, she had been doing that work she had come here to do.

Nancy's second life lesson activation came when she lost her son from a brain tumor in his twenties. This was the completion of her secondary life lesson of Acceptance. This was the gift he gave to her that shifted everything for Nancy. She has had a difficult life, married to an alcoholic, she had to learn to practice patience, acceptance, tolerance, understanding, and to love unconditionally without judgment. When she talks of her marriage now it is with a smile on her face and unconditional love in her heart. She remembers good times and laughs about the difficult ones.

I have done several sessions with Nancy over the many years I have known her. They are always very enjoyable for me, as they are different than most other sessions I do. Because of the level at which she herself operates, we quickly reach very deep understandings. In reality, if I tried to do a session with her in the normal way she wouldn't have the time or patience for it. I usually feel like my sessions with Nancy are a waste of time for her, but she clearly cherishes the hours we spend together. I think I stimulate her. More than anything else I feel that I am putting words to truths that she already knows. In this way we seem to validate each other, which is probably why we still continue to do sessions together.

Up to this point in time, Nancy's own writings have sat largely unpublished as she is simply too far ahead of her time for others to comprehend. The greatest challenge for anyone working with the life lesson of Grace is to learn to accept that very few people can grasp the deep Universal truths that they know and yet cannot express in words.

It may sound as though a life lesson of Grace is a special one that everyone wants to claim as their own. I can tell you that it is a very unique experience that is not tolerable by most. I have no doubt that Nancy is a last-timer. To be truthful, I actually think she has been a last-timer several times over.   She has a deep itch that has yet to be scratched, and until she understands *everything* she will undoubtedly keep coming back.

Interestingly enough, Nancy's mother always told her that she should have been named Grace.

Chapter 8

Conclusion

_____

In understanding the larger picture of our experience as spirits in human form it is helpful to keep in mind that we are not here to learn lessons *per se*. In fact, it may even be said that the Twelve Primary Life Lessons themselves are only a distraction to keep us busy while we are learning the larger attribute that encompasses our spiritual beings. To put it simply, what we are really here to learn is the Art of Mastery itself. The definition of Mastery is finding positive uses for all energy in all situations. When we attain this, we will finally remember our true power as Creators.

We are experiencing an evolution on a scale never before seen. I truly believe that when we look back on this time two hundred years hence, we will clearly see that humanity went through an exceptionally rapid evolutionary jump. This is what we are in the middle of right now. These are exciting times indeed, and they will only become even more exciting as we move forward.

You can easily see that even though this information and these life lessons have been around since the beginning of this wondrous game we are playing, they have been so obscure that it would have been futile to make this information known any earlier. If a soul averaged 60 lifetimes to master a single life lesson this information would have been meaningless on a day to day basis. We would be – and indeed were - so wrapped up in our need for survival we would have no interest in life lessons.

What's Next?

With our evolutionary process now on such a fast track it is quite natural for us to immediately want to take this information to the next evolutionary step as well. The next questions then become: where are we going? And, what is ahead with the Twelve Primary Life Lessons?

I believe that the Twelve Primary Life Lessons will remain relatively unchanged. After all, they have served us very well from early caveman times to the present day. What I do see changing is the relationship we have to the seven stages of life. Obviously, as we increase our longevity, the age parameters for each stage will also change. More importantly, I actually believe that there is another change that is beginning to take place. Among the spiritual community, this change is being defined as ascension. From the Group's point of view, ascension does not mean leaving our physical bodies to go on to a higher plane of existence. Rather, ascension actually requires us to start the life process over again, while remaining in physical form. Thus, the direction I believe we will eventually take is one in which we start the seven stages of life over again within the same single lifetime.

I am not going to explain this any further in this volume. What I will do, however, is give you a clue as to how this may play out. Imagine taking all of your life experiences one by one, and then deciding which ones you want to keep with you and carry forward into your next lifetime, and which ones you would rather release. Up until now, this is what we have always done in the seventh stage of life, which occurs after death.

Imagine what it will be like when it becomes possible for us to plan our next incarnation and set up all the necessary contracts without even having to leave one's present life behind. Would this not be the most exciting, evolutionary leap ever?

This is no pipe dream or idle conjecture. This is what I fervently believe is the next step for mankind. To take this one stage further, I am even willing to bet that we will see the early evidence of this during my own lifetime.

Furthermore, I also believe that the children now entering our world with higher attributes than previous generations will be the ones that will activate our full potential to do exactly this. Make no mistake, the Indigo and Crystal Children now entering our world will catapult humanity forward in a way that we are only just beginning to get a glimpse of.

Yes, indeed, this is the most exciting time to be on Earth.

In this book I have presented a great deal of information to help you view life from a different perspective. I have approached the human experience from a spiritual standpoint, for this is the way this information was presented to me by the Group. Please keep in mind that this work is all about empowerment. Therefore, my greatest hope is that you will not take everything presented here as the *only* truth. Instead, I ask that you run everything through your own filters and take only those parts that resonate within your own heart. This is the very essence of discernment. This is the foundation of all the information that comes from the Group. Even if you take only one piece of information that assists you and your clients to dance in your passion and play in your joy, then I will have fulfilled my purpose in writing this book.

In the final analysis, always re-member, life is a wonderful game and the purpose of playing it is to give us a chance to experience our passion and joy!

About the Author

Steve Rother was comfortably settled into life as a General Building Contractor in the San Diego area when, through a synchronistic series of events, he was placed firmly in the middle of his life contract. Steve and his wife Barbara began shifting their focus on life and living on New Year's, 1995, when they found themselves unexpectedly expressing their intent for the coming year during a ceremony that took place as the sun rose over a California beach. Steve began receiving divinely inspired messages about human evolution and how we can all experience an empowered life style. From that day forward, their lives were never to be the same.

Today, the source of this divinely inspired information is known simply as the Group. They offer practical information on leading empowered lives as evolving humans. This divine information has filled three books to date, and there are five more currently in the making. The monthly messages distributed over the internet, along with the books are translated into 18 languages each month. Steve and Barbara travel extensively presenting seminars on a global basis and are five time presenters to charters of the United Nations on two Continents.

Steve and Barbara make their base in San Diego, California, where they have formed the nonprofit corporation of Lightworker. Together with the volunteers and staff of the Lightworker organization they plant seeds of Light through personal empowerment on a global basis. More information about Lightworker, Steve, Barbara and the Group, including their seminar schedule, can be found at the Lightworker web site: http://www.lightworker.com